# *A Part of Speech*

BY JOSEPH BRODSKY

*Elegy for John Donne and Other Poems*

*Selected Poems*

*A Part of Speech*

*Less Than One*

*To Urania*

*Marbles*

# A PART OF SPEECH

# JOSEPH BRODSKY

*The Noonday Press*
*Farrar, Straus and Giroux*
*New York*

*Translation copyright © 1973, 1974, 1976, 1977,*
*1978, 1979, 1980 by Farrar, Straus and Giroux, Inc.*
*Originally published in Russian, in* ОСТАНОВКА В ПУСТЫНЕ,
*© 1970 by Chekhov Publishing Corporation; and in*
КОНЕЦ ПРЕКРАСНОЙ ЭПОХИ *and* ЧАСТЬ РЕЧИ,
*© 1977 by Joseph Brodsky*
*All rights reserved*
*Published in Canada by HarperCollinsCanadaLtd*
*Printed in the United States of America*
*First edition, 1980*
*Fifth printing, 1991*

*Library of Congress Cataloging in Publication Data*
*Brodskiĭ, Iosif   /   A part of speech.*
*Translation of Chast' rechi.*
*Includes bibliographical references.*
*I.   Title.*
*PG3479.4.R64C4513 1980   891.71'44   80–613*

Some of these poems first appeared, in somewhat different form,
in *The New Yorker, The New York Review of Books,
Bananas, Confrontation, The Iowa Review, The Kenyon
Review, The Los Angeles Times, Paintbrush,* and *Vogue.*
Grateful acknowledgment is made for permission to
reprint from: *Kontinent* edited by Vladimir Maximov,
Doubleday & Co., Inc., translation © 1976 by André
Deutsch Limited and Doubleday & Co., Inc.; *Joseph
Brodsky: Selected Poems,* translated by George L.
Kline, Harper & Row, Publishers, Inc., translation and
introduction © 1973 by George L. Kline; *The Mind-Reader*
by Richard Wilbur, Harcourt Brace Jovanovich, Inc.,
translation © 1975 by Richard Wilbur

*The text of this book was developed with
the editorial counsel of Barry Rubin*

*To my mother and father*

———————————————————

Since a translation, by definition, lags behind the original work, a good number of poems included in this collection belong chronologically in *Selected Poems*, published in 1973. The reason for my putting them into this book, however, is not so much a desire to provide the reader with the complete picture as an attempt to supply this book with a semblance of context, with a sense of continuum.

I would like to thank each of my translators for his long hours of work in rendering my poems into English. I have taken the liberty of reworking some of the translations to bring them closer to the original, though perhaps at the expense of their smoothness. I am doubly grateful to the translators for their indulgence.

My thanks also to Ann Frydman, Masha Vorobiova, and Stephen White for preparing interlinear versions for this book. And I gratefully acknowledge my debt to Jonathan Aaron, Nancy Meiselas, Margo Picken, David Rieff, Pat Strachan, Peter Viereck, and, above all, to Barry Rubin and Derek Walcott, for their suggestions, proofreading, and assistance with certain references. My special thanks go to the John Simon Guggenheim Foundation, which made it possible for me to complete this collection.

J.B.

# Contents

## A Song to No Music

Six Years Later | 3

Anno Domini | 5

Autumn in Norenskaya | 8

A second Christmas | 10

Homage to Yalta | 11

A Song to No Music | 26

The End of a Beautiful Era | 34

Lithuanian Divertissement | 37

On Love | 40

I Sit by the Window | 41

Nature Morte | 43

December 24, 1971 | 47

To a Tyrant | 49

The Funeral of Bobò | 50

Letters to a Roman Friend | 52

Nunc Dimittis | 55

Odysseus to Telemachus | 58

## A Part of Speech

An autumn evening | 61

1972 | 63

*In the Lake District | 67*

*The Butterfly | 68*

*Torso | 73*

*Lagoon | 74*

*The classical ballet | 77*

*On the Death of Zhukov | 78*

*Mexican Divertimento | 79*

*The Thames at Chelsea | 89*

*A Part of Speech | 92*

*Lullaby of Cape Cod | 107*

*December in Florence | 119*

*In England | 122*

*Plato Elaborated | 129*

*Letters from the Ming Dynasty | 132*

*The Rustle of Acacias | 134*

*Elegy: for Robert Lowell | 135*

*Strophes | 138*

*San Pietro | 145*

NOTES | *149*

# A Song to No Music

# Six Years Later

So long had life together been that now
the second of January fell again
on Tuesday, making her astonished brow
lift like a windshield wiper in the rain,
    so that her misty sadness cleared, and showed
    a cloudless distance waiting up the road.

So long had life together been that once
the snow began to fall, it seemed unending;
that, lest the flakes should make her eyelids wince,
I'd shield them with my hand, and they, pretending
    not to believe that cherishing of eyes,
    would beat against my palm like butterflies.

So alien had all novelty become
that sleep's entanglements would put to shame
whatever depths the analysts might plumb;
that when my lips blew out the candle flame,
    her lips, fluttering from my shoulder, sought
    to join my own, without another thought.

So long had life together been that all
that tattered brood of papered roses went,
and a whole birch grove grew upon the wall,
and we had money, by some accident,
    and tonguelike on the sea, for thirty days,
    the sunset threatened Turkey with its blaze.

So long had life together been without
books, chairs, utensils—only that ancient bed—
that the triangle, before it came about,
had been a perpendicular, the head
    of some acquaintance hovering above
    two points which had been coalesced by love.

So long had life together been that she
and I, with our joint shadows, had composed
a double door, a door which, even if we
were lost in work or sleep, was always closed:
      somehow its halves were split and we went right
      through them into the future, into night.

*1969  /  Translated by Richard Wilbur*

# *Anno Domini*

The provinces are celebrating Christmas.
The Governor-general's mansion is bedecked
with mistletoe, torches smoke by the entrance.
In the lanes the people press and lark around.
A merry, idle, dirty, boisterous
throng crowds in the rear of the mansion.

The Governor-general is ill. He lies
on a couch, wrapped in a shawl from Alcazar,
where he once served, and his thoughts turn
on his wife and on his secretary
receiving guests downstairs in the hall.
He is not really jealous. At this moment

it's more important to him to retire
into his shell of illness, dreams, the deferment of
his transfer to the capital. And since
he knows that freedom is not needed
by the crowd at all to make a public holiday—
for this same reason he allows

even his wife to be unfaithful. What would
he think of if ennui attacks
did not plague him? If he loved?
A chilly tremor runs through his shoulders,
he chases these alarming thoughts away.
In the hall the merrymaking subsides

but does not end. Muddled with drink,
the leaders of the tribes stare glassily
into a distance now devoid of enemies.
Their teeth, expressive of their rage,
set in a smile that's like a wheel
held fast by brakes—and a servant

is loading them with food. In his sleep
a merchant cries out. Snatches of song are heard.
The Governor-general's wife and secretary
slip out into the garden. And on the wall
the imperial eagle, like a bat, stares down,
having gorged on the Governor-general's liver.

And I, a writer who has seen the world,
who has crossed the equator on an ass,
look out of the window at the hills asleep
and think about the identity of our woes:
the Emperor won't see him, I won't be
seen by my son and Cynthia . . . And we,

we here shall perish. Arrogance will not raise
our bitter fate to the level of proof
that we are made in the Creator's image.
The grave will render all alike.
So, if only in our lifetime, let us be various!
For what reason should we rush from the mansion,

we cannot judge our homeland. The sword of justice
will stick fast in our personal disgrace:
the heirs, the power, are in stronger hands . . .
How good that vessels are not sailing!
How good that the sea is freezing!
How good that the birds in the clouds

are too frail for such cumbrous frames!
For that, nobody is to blame.
But perhaps our weights will be
proportionate exactly to their voices.
Therefore, let them fly to our homeland.
Therefore, let them yell out to us.

My country . . . foreign gentlemen,
visiting Cynthia, are leaning
over the crib like latter-day magi.
The infant slumbers. A star glimmers
like a coal under a cold font.
And the visitors, not touching his head,

replace the halo by an aureole of lies,
and the Virgin Birth by gossip,
by the passing over of the father in silence  . . .
The mansion empties. The lights on each floor die.
First one, then another. Finally, the last.
And only two windows in the whole palace

are alight: mine, where, with my back to the torchlight,
I watch the moon's disk glide
over the sparsely growing trees, and see
Cynthia, the snow; the Governor-general's, where
he struggles silently all night with his illness
and keeps the fire lit, to see his enemy.

The enemy withdraws. The faint light of day
barely breaking in the world's East,
creeps through the window, straining
to see what is happening within,
and, coming across the remnants of the feast,
falters. But continues on its way.

*Palanga, 1968  /  Translated by Daniel Weissbort*

# *Autumn in Norenskaya*

We return from the field. The wind
clangs buckets upturned,
unbraids the willow fringe,
whistles through boulder piles.
The horses, inflated casks
of ribs trapped between shafts,
snap at the rusted harrows
with gnashing profiles.

A gust combs frostbitten sorrel,
bloats kerchiefs and shawls, searches
up the skirts of old hags, scrolls them
tight up as cabbageheads.
Eyes lowered, hacking out phlegm,
the women scissor their way home,
like cutting along a dull hem,
lurch toward their wooden beds.

Between folds flash the thighs of scissors,
wet eyes blur with the vision
of crabbed little imps that dance on
the farm women's pupils as a shower flings
the semblance of faces against a bare
pane. The furrows fan out in braids
under the harrow. The wind breaks
a chain of crows into shrieking links.

These visions are the final sign
of an inner life that seizes on
any specter to which it feels kin
till the specter scares off for good
at the church bell of a creaking axle,
at the metal rattle of the world as it
lies reversed in a rut of water,
at a starling soaring into cloud.

The sky lowers. The shouldered rake
sees the damp roofs first, staked
out against the ridge of a dark
hill that's just a mound far off.
Three versts still to cover. Rain
lords it over this beaten plain,
and to the crusted boots cling brown
stubborn clods of the native earth.

*1965  /  Translated by Daniel Weissbort with the author*

A second Christmas by the shore
of Pontus, which remains unfrozen.
The Star of Kings above the sharp horizon
of harbor walls. And I can't say for sure
that I can't live without you. As
this paper proves, I do exist: I'm living
enough to gulp my beer, to soil the leaves, and
trample the grass.

Retreating south before winter's assault,
I sit in that café from which we two were
exploded soundlessly into the future
according to the unrelenting law
that happiness can't last. My finger tries
your face on poor man's marble. In the distance,
brocaded nymphs leap through their jerky dances,
flaunting their thighs.

Just what, you gods—if this dilating blot,
glimpsed through a murky window, symbolizes
your selves now—were you trying to advise us?
The future has arrived and it is not
unbearable. Things fall, the fiddler goes,
the music ebbs, and deepening creases
spread over the sea's surface and men's faces.
But no wind blows.

Someday the slowly rising breakers but,
alas, not we, will sweep across this railing,
crest overhead, crush helpless screams, and roll in
to find the spot where you drank wine, took cat-
naps, spreading to the sun your wet
thin blouse—to batter benches, splinter boardwalks,
and build for future molluscs
a silted bed.

*Yalta, 1971* / *Translated by George L. Kline*

# Homage to Yalta

The story to be told below is truthful.
Unfortunately, nowadays it's not
just lies alone but simple truth as well
that needs compelling argument and sound
corroboration. Isn't that a sign
of our arrival in a wholly new
but doleful world? In fact, a proven truth,
to be precise, is not a truth at all—
it's just the sum of proofs. But now
what's said is "I agree," not "I believe."

What troubles people in the atom age is—
much less than things themselves—the way they are
constructed. Like a child who clobbers dolly,
then wails on finding the debris inside,
we tend to take what lies in back of this
or that event as nothing less than that
event itself. To which there is a kind
of fascination, inasmuch as things
like motives, attitudes, environment,
et cetera—all this is life. And life
we have been trained to treat as if it were
the object of our logical deductions.

And sometimes all it seems we have to do
is interweave them—motives, attitudes,
environment, and problems—and events
will then take place; a crime, let's say. But no.
It's just an ordinary day out there.
It's drizzling, cars go rushing by. Inside,
a standard-model telephone (a clump
of cathodes, junctions, terminals, resistors)
is resolutely speechless. No event,
alas, takes place. On second thought, thank God.

The matter here described occurred in Yalta.
Of course, I'll make an effort to comply with
the view of truth I mentioned earlier—
that is to say, I plan to disembowel
that dolly. But I hope you will forgive
me, gentle reader, if I here and there
append to truth an element of Art,
which, in the last analysis, lies at
the heart of all events (though, to be sure,
a writer's art is not the Art of life,
it only forms a likeness).
                              Testimony
of witnesses will follow in the order
in which it was obtained. Herein lies an
example of how truth depends on art,
and not of art's dependence on the truth.


                              I
"He telephoned that evening and he said
he wasn't coming. He and I beforehand,
on Tuesday, had agreed that he'd drop by
my place on Saturday. Yes, yes, on Tuesday.
I'd called him and invited him to come.
'On Saturday' is when he said he'd see me.
The purpose? Simply that for quite a while
we'd hoped to sit and analyze together
a problem of Chigorin's. That was all.
Our meeting was to have no other 'purpose,'
to use your word. Unless, of course, you choose
to say that wishing to take pleasure in a
congenial person's company amounts to
a purpose. Still, you probably know better . . .
As luck would have it, though, he phoned that evening
and said he'd not be coming. What a shame
it was! I really would have liked to see him.
Distraught? Was that the word you used? Oh, no.
He sounded just the same as usual. But
of course, a telephone's a telephone;
although, you know, when you can't see a person
you focus on his voice a bit more sharply.
He didn't sound distraught . . . But then, the way

he phrased his words was always somewhat odd.
His speech consisted, on the whole, of pauses
that always made you feel uneasy, since
we ordinarily interpret silence
to mean a person's mind is busy working.
And his, in fact, was nothing but pure silence.
You'd soon begin to get a feeling of
your own dependence on this quietness,
and that would irritate a lot of people.
Oh, no, I knew it had resulted from
his shell shock. Yes, of that I'm very certain.
How else would you explain the fact . . . What's that?
That's right, he didn't sound at all distraught. But
of course, that's only judging by his voice.
There is one thing I'll say in any case:
that Saturday and earlier, on Tuesday,
he sounded just the same as usual. So
if something really happened to him then,
it wasn't Saturday, because he called!
That simply doesn't fit distraught behavior!
Take me: when I'm distraught, for instance . . .What?
The tenor of our conversation? Gladly.
The moment that I heard the telephone I
was there to pick it up. 'Good evening, it
is I; I owe you an apology. For,
as things turn out, I simply won't be able
to come today.' Oh, really? That's a shame.
On Wednesday, maybe? Should I call you up?
Offended? Why, for heaven's sake, of course not!
Until next Wednesday, then? 'Good night,' he answered.
That's right, it was at eight or thereabout.
When I hung up I cleared away the dishes
and took the board out. Last time, his advice
had been to try the Queen E-8 maneuver.
An odd and somewhat muddled move it was.
Nonsensical, almost. And not at all in
the spirit of Chigorin. Odd it was,
and senseless. Didn't change a thing, and therefore
it nullified the meaning of the problem.
In any game what matters are results:
a win, a loss, or even if a draw—

but nonetheless an outcome. His move, though—
it seemed as if it put the pieces in
some doubt about their very own existence.
I sat up with the board till late at night.
Perhaps the game may someday actually
be played like that. As far as I'm concerned,
however . . . Sorry, what was that you asked: does
the name mean anything to me? It does.
Five years ago the two of us broke up.
Yes, that's correct: we weren't ever married.
Was he aware of it? Most likely not.
It surely wasn't something she'd have told him.
What's that? This photograph? I'd make a point
of putting it away before he came here.
Oh, no! You needn't be apologetic.
The question is quite natural, and I . . .
How was it that I knew about the murder?
I got a call from her that very night.
Now there's a voice that really was distraught!"

## II

"Last year I didn't see him very often,
but still, I saw him. Twice a month he'd pay
a visit, sometimes even not that often.
Except October, when he never came at all.
He'd usually call to let me know
ahead of time. A week or so beforehand.
In order to avoid a mix-up. I'm,
you know, in theater. Something unexpected
is always coming up. For instance, all
at once, a person's taken ill or leaves us
to make a film—and has to be replaced.
Well, basically, that sort of thing. Besides that—
besides, he knew that now I had become . . .
Why, yes. That's right. But how on earth did you know?
But after all, that is your métier.
However, this time things are, well, I'd say it's
a serious involvement. What I mean
by that is . . . Yes, and all that notwithstanding,
I still continued seeing him. Oh, how
can I explain it! He was rather odd, I

would say, and not like anyone. Of course,
yes, everyone is different from all others.
But he was very different from us all.
Yes, that's precisely what I found attractive.
When we were with each other, all around
us everything would cease existing. I mean
it all continued moving and revolving—
the world went on, he didn't block it out.
Love? No, that's not what all this talk has been
about! The world went on. But suddenly
the top of things—both moving and immobile—
was covered with a sort of film or, rather,
a coat of dust, which gave them all a kind
of senseless similarity. For instance,
you know, the way they paint the walls and ceilings
and beds all white in hospitals. All right, then.
Now try to form a picture of my room
all blanketed with snow. Peculiar, wouldn't
you say? But at the same time, don't you think
that furniture would only stand to gain
from such a metamorphosis? You don't? That's
a shame. Back then I used to think that sameness
was in reality the world's true surface.
I valued that sensation very dearly.
Yes, that's exactly why I never broke
things off. Just why should I have had to,
pray tell me, sever our relations? Should I
have left him for the captain's sake? Well, frankly,
that's not the way I see it. Certainly, he's
an earnest sort of person, even if
he is an officer. However, what
means most to me is that sensation! Really,
could he have given it to me? O God! I'm
beginning only now to understand
just how important that sensation was
to me! And furthermore, it's so peculiar.
Specifically? The fact that I myself
will now be just another tiny speck in
the universe. I, too, will now be tinged
with that same patina. And all the while I'll
be thinking I'm not like the rest! . . . Until

we realize that we can be repeated,
we don't know anything. It's awful, awful.

Forgive me while I pour myself some wine.
And some for you? With pleasure. Don't be silly,
I won't think anything at all! Just when
and where was it we met? I don't remember.
I guess it was the beach. That's right, it was:
Livadia—we met there on the beach of
the health resort. Where else do people get
together in a hole like ours? But really,
you do know all about me, don't you! Still,
I know you'd never guess the words with which
we first became acquainted. What he said was,
'I'm sure you find me quite obnoxious, but . . .'
The rest of what he said is not important.
A pretty good beginning, don't you think?
If I were you, I'd add it to my stock
of weapons. I can say that as a woman.
What do I know about his family?
Why, absolutely nothing. Well, I think he . . .
he evidently had a son—but where?
On second thought that's wrong, I've got it twisted:
the child's the captain's. Yes, a kid, a schoolboy.
Morose; but on the whole the image of
his father . . . No, I haven't got the slightest
idea about his family—or friends.
As I recall, he never introduced me
to anyone. Forgive me while I have
a little more. You're right: the evening's stifling.

No, I don't know who killed him. What was that?
You must be kidding! He's a total washout.
The man was driven crazy by queen's gambits.
Besides, the two of them were friends. Now that
was something I could not explain: their friendship.
Inside that club of theirs they smoke so much
they easily can stink the whole South Shore up.
Why, no, the captain spent the evening at the
performance. Yes, of course, in mufti. I
can't stand their uniform. And afterward we

returned together.
                    We found him there
at my front entrance. He was lying in
the doorway. 'Just a drunk,' was our assumption.
You see, our hall is rather dark. But then
I recognized the raincoat he was wearing.
The coat was white but smeared with mud. No, no,
that's right, he didn't drink. I know for certain.
Yes, evidently he'd been crawling. And
for quite a while. What then? Well, first we brought
him into my place, then we rang up the
police. Not me, the captain. I felt ill.

Yes, this whole thing's a real nightmare. Oh,
you think so, too? I find that so surprising.
You know: it is your job and all. You're right,
I'm sure it's hard to get accustomed to it.
You're human, too, of course . . . I'm sorry!
I didn't put that very nicely . . . Yes,
please pour yourself another; none for me, though.
I've had enough. What's more, I haven't slept
well lately and rehearsal's in the morning.
Well, if it helps insomnia. You're certain?
In that case, just a swallow. Yes, you're right,
the atmosphere tonight is really stifling.
Oppressive, too. There's absolutely nothing
to breathe. Oh—everything just makes it hard.
The stuffiness. I'm suffocating. Yes.
And you? And you? You, too? You, too, then? Nothing—
there's nothing else at all I know. Oh, yes?
There's absolutely nothing I can tell you.
Say, what is it you want from me? What is it . . .
All right, now. Tell me, huh? What is it? What?"

                    III
"It's your opinion, then, that I'm obliged to
provide you explanations? Well, all right,
if I'm obliged, then I'm obliged. But mind you:
I'm bound to disappoint you inasmuch
as I most certainly know less about him
than you do. Even that much is enough, though,

to drive a person mad. But I suppose
that's not a threat to you, since you are  . . .  Yes,
that's absolutely true: I couldn't stomach
the character. I think you know the reasons.
And if you don't—it makes no sense at all
to get involved in explanations. That
especially holds true since in the end
what interests you are facts. So there you have it:
I openly admit it—I despised him.

No, he and I had never met. I knew—
I knew that someone used to see her. Only
I didn't know exactly who, though. She,
of course, did not say anything to me. But
I knew! One didn't have to be a Sherlock
like you to know it. Average concern
was really all it took. Especially since  . . .
But you don't know the sort of person she is!
Although she didn't talk about the guy,
that doesn't mean that she was hiding something!
She simply didn't want to see me get
upset—that's all it was. And anyway, there
was nothing, after all, to hide. As she
herself admitted when I cornered her, it
has almost been a year since anything
went on between them  . . .  What was that? I don't
quite understand. Did I believe her? Sure, I
believed her. Whether that was any consolation
is, frankly speaking, something else entirely.

You may in fact be right. It's easier
for you to tell. But if a person says a thing,
it's not because he wants to be distrusted.
To me, the very movement in itself
of someone's lips is even more essential
than truth or falsehood; just the very movement
of lips contains more life than do the words
the lips are moved by. I have said that I
believed her. No! A certain something else was
involved. It's simply that I saw what she
was telling me. (I didn't hear it, mind you;

instead, I saw it. ) Try to understand:
Before my eyes there stood a human being—
a speaking, breathing, moving human being.
I didn't want to think it all a lie,
nor could I . . . you're amazed that even with an
approach like that I somehow still was able
to get four stars? They're very little stars, though.
I started out quite differently. The ones
who started with me have been wearing big stars
a long, long time already. Many even
have two. (In your account of this whole thing
be sure to add that I'm a failure, too; it
will help to make it sound more plausible.) I
repeat: I started differently. Like you, I
kept looking for skulduggery around
me everywhere. And, naturally, I'd find it.
It's in a soldier's blood: they're always out
to put one over on the brass . . . But then
one day in Košice, in '44, I
discovered this was stupid. Twenty-eight
of them were lying in the snow before
me, men I hadn't trusted—soldiers.
What? Why do I discuss this if it has
no bearing on the matter? I was only
attempting to reply to what you asked.

Yes, I'm a widower. It's been four years now.
Yes, I have children. One, that is. A son.
Where was I in the evening Saturday? At
the theater. Afterward, I took her home.
Yes, he was lying there at her front entrance.
What? How did I react then? Not at all.
Of course, I recognized him. I had seen them
together once in the department store. They
were in the midst of buying something. That
was when I understood . . .
                              The fact is, we'd
run into one another now and then on
the beach. We both preferred the same location:
that spot—remember?—over by the fence.
And on his neck I'd always see those bruises . . .

the ones . . . oh, you know . . . So, then. Once
I spoke to him—most likely it was something
about the weather. Quickly he leaned over
in my direction and without a glance
at me he said: 'I just don't feel like talking . . .'
and only after several seconds passed
he added on: '. . . to you.' And all the while he
kept looking upward into space. Right then,
I swear to you, I could have murdered him.
My vision blurred, and everything was swimming.
I felt a scalding wave go rising through
my brain, and momentarily I think I
lost consciousness. When I regained my senses,
he'd reassumed that previous repose
of his, and then he'd covered up his face with
a newspaper. And meanwhile, on his neck I
could clearly see those marks—those darkish bruises . . .
No, I was not aware of who in fact
he was then. Luckily, I'd not yet met her.

What then? Well, then I think he disappeared;
I somehow never saw him any more at
the beach. And then an officers' reception
was given at the club, and that was when
I met her. Later on I saw them there—in
the store . . . and that was why I recognized him
at once that night, on Saturday. To tell you
the honest truth, in some way I was glad.
It might have otherwise gone on forever,
and every time, just following his visits,
she wasn't quite herself. But now I hope
that things will soon be going as they ought to.
At first it's bound to be a little hard,
but I for one can tell you: in the end
the murdered are forgotten. And, moreover,
it looks like we'll be leaving. I've been called
to the Academy. That's right, in Kiev.
Why, any theater there will hire her. And
my son is very friendly with her. Who
can tell? It's possible we'll have a child of
our own. As you can see, I'm—ha, ha, ha—

still . . . Yes, I do possess a handgun.
No, no, it's not a Stechkin; only my
old trophy from the war—a Parabellum.
Well, yes, I know the wound was from a gunshot."

IV

"That evening Pop shoved off and headed for
the theater. I stayed home myself with Grannie.
Uh-huh, the two of us watched television.
My homework? It was Saturday, remember.
So we watched television. What was on?
I'm not so sure now. Maybe it was Sorge.
Yeah, Sorge, right! I didn't watch it to
the end, though. I had seen the thing already.
Our class once took a trip to see the film.
That's all . . . At what point did I go away?
Oh, at the part with Klausen and the Germans.
I mean, it was the Japs . . . and then they still
keep going in that boat along the shoreline.
Yes, it was sometime after nine o'clock.
For sure. I know because on Saturday
the supermarket closes up at ten, and
I felt like having ice cream. No, I looked
out through the window—after all, it's only
across the street. That's right, and then I felt
like walking. No, I didn't mention it
to Grannie. Why? She would have started in
about a coat and hat and gloves—and that sort
of thing. Uh-huh, I wore a jacket. Not on
your life, not this; I wore my hooded one.
It's got a zipper.
                    Yes, I put it in
my pocket. No, no, no. I simply knew where
he kept the key . . . Sure, just for fun, of course!
No, not to be a show-off. Who would I have
shown off to? Late? Yes, right, and very dark.
What thoughts I had? I wasn't even thinking.
I guess that all I did was walk and walk.

Huh? How was it I ended up there?
I don't remember . . . Well, I guess, because—as

[ 21 ]

you walk downhill the harbor always stays
in front of you. And so do lights in port.
Yeah, that's a fact, and you can try and picture
what's going on there. Anyhow, when you're
already on your way back home, it's nicer
to go downhill. Yes, quiet, and the moon
was out. Well, mostly, it was really gorgeous.
Pass by? No, no one happened to pass by me.
Not really, no. I didn't know the time. But
on Saturdays the *Pushkin* sails at midnight.
It hadn't left yet, though. Down there, astern,
they've got a lounge for dancing, and the windows
are stained glass. When you're way up there they look like
they're emeralds. Yeah, and then . . .
                              I what? Of course not!
Her place is up above the park, while I,
I met him at the park, right by the exit.
Do what? Oh, tell you how I feel about her
in general? Oh, well, I guess—I think
she's very pretty. Yeah, and so does Grannie.
And, well, she's sort of nice, she doesn't bug you.
It's all the same, though; I don't really care.
Oh, Dad'll work it out  . . .
                              Yes, at the entrance.
Yeah, he was smoking. Sure, I asked for one,
but he refused and then  . . .  Well, anyway, so
he said to me, 'Come on, now, beat it, willya?!'
A minute later—after I had walked
away about ten steps, or maybe farther—
beneath his breath he added, 'Scoundrel.' It
was very quiet then and so I heard him.
I really don't know what came over me!
Uh-huh, it felt like I'd been hit by someone.
And things began to swim before my eyes—
honestly I don't remember turning
and firing at him! But I know I missed:
he still was standing where he'd been before, and
I think he still was smoking. Then I . . . then . . .
I started screaming and I ran as fast as hell.
But he . . . well, he was standing there and . . .
                              No one

had ever talked to me like that before!
So tell me: what was it I'd done? Just asked
for one. All right, a cigarette. So what if
it was? I know that smoking's bad. Yeah, sure,
but almost everybody smokes. And, really,
I didn't even feel like smoking! No,
I didn't plan to smoke it. All I wanted
to do was hold it . . . No! No, no! I didn't.
I didn't want to look grown up. I said
I wouldn't have! But there, down in the harbor,
the lights were everywhere, like fireflies, too,
at anchorage . . . and here it also would've . . .
I can't explain it right . . . If you can help it—
please, don't tell Pop! He'll kill me . . . Yes, exactly.
I put it back. No, Grannie was already
asleep. She hadn't even turned the set off.
The lines were flickering . . . Immediately,
I put it back immediately. Then I
got into bed! Don't tell my pop about it!
He'd murder me! Well, anyhow, I missed!
I missed—I didn't hit him, did I? Did I?!"

V

Name: such and such. Born: forty years ago.
State nationality. Unmarried. Children:
write "none." Preceding place of residence.
Is registered to live in. Where and when and
by whom deceased was found. List suspects.
As follows: three. So there it is—three suspects.
In general, the simple fact that one can
suspect three people of a murder is
extremely telling. Yes, unquestionably,
three people can perform the selfsame act.
Consume a roasted chicken, for example.
But this is murder. And the very fact that
suspicion fell on all of them provides
a guaranty that any of the suspects
was capable of murder. Consequently,
the whole investigation loses meaning—
because an inquest only tells you who
it was, but not that others couldn't do it . . .

[ 23 ]

Oh, come now! No! Get goose bumps? Fiddlesticks!
But on the whole, a man's ability to
commit a murder and, again, a man's
ability to probe it—even though there
exists a patent continuity
between them—aren't equivalent. That's certain.
Most likely, it's the impact of their closeness . . .
Oh, yes, indeed, it is—the whole affair's
lamentable . . .
     What's that? What's that you're saying?
You think the number in itself of those
on whom suspicion fell specifically
unites them, as it were, and in addition
in some way functions as an alibi?
That we can't hope to feed three people on
one chicken? Undeniably. And, as it
turns out, the murderer is not encompassed
within that circle, he's outside it. That
he's one of those who aren't in fact suspected!?
In other words, the murderer's the one
who doesn't have a motive for the murder!?
Yes, that's the way it happened this time. Yes,
you're quite correct . . . But that's . . .
        why, that's . . . it's simply
an apologia for the absurd. An
apotheosis of the meaningless!
Delirium! So it turns out, then, that
it's logical. Hold on! Explain to me
the meaning of existence. Not a boy
emerging from the bushes in a jacket
who opens fire on you?! But if it's—if it's
so, why do we consider this a crime? And what
is more, investigate it! What a nightmare.
It turns out all our lives we're waiting to
be murdered, and thereby investigating
just proves to be a form of expectation,
and furthermore a criminal's not even
a criminal, and . . .
    Sorry, I feel sick.
Come, let's go up on deck; it's stifling in here . . .
That's Yalta, yes. You see that—over there—

that building? No, a little higher, next to
the Monument . . . Just look how it's lit up!
It's pretty, isn't it? No, I can't tell you
how long they'll give him. No, that part of it
is not our business. It's the court's. Most likely
they'll give him . . . Sorry, at the moment I'm
not capable of focusing attention
on punishment. I just can't seem to breathe.
It's nothing, it'll pass. Yes, out at sea it
is sure to ease a bit. Livadia?
Right there. Yes, yes, that group of lights. Chic, isn't
it? Even in the night . . . I didn't hear you.
Yes, right, thank God. At last we're under way.

As the *Kolkhida* stirred a backwash, Yalta—
replete with all its flowers, palm trees, lights, and
vacationers still clinging to the doors of
already closed establishments, like flies
to lighted lamps—deliberately rolled
and started heaving to. A night above
the sea is different from a night above
dry land in just about the way a gaze
encountered in a mirror differs from
a gaze directed at another person . . .
And the *Kolkhida* put to sea. Astern
it left a foamy, hissing wake, and in
the midnight darkness the peninsula
was gradually melting. More precisely,
it was returning to the boundaries
of which our maps incessantly remind us.

*1969 / Translated by Barry Rubin*

# A Song to No Music

[ *For Faith Wigzell* ]

When you recall me in that land,
although this phrase isn't oracular—
a fact unthinkable for an
eye armed with tears as its binocular—

but just a fantasy whose string's
too limp for fishing out the very
date of this great event from ink-
like ponds of counting days; so when you,

beyond all seven seas, beyond
those lands whose sum is hardly shorter,
may, after all, recall me (though
I stress again: tears shrink the order

of everything except bygones)
nostalgically, in that Lord's summer,
and when you duly sigh (oh, don't
sigh), pondering the blinding number

of seas and fields flung out between
us, won't you notice something sadder:
i.e., the thing which led that train
of zeros was yourself.
                         A matter
quite likely of your hubris or,
more likely, of my own delusions,
or of the time not ripe yet for
our jumping to some brave conclusions:

still, it's surprising that a man
who fared so poorly as your guardian
against much lesser evils can
relieve you from this sighing burden.

The future is a form of dark;
compare it to a midnight's quiet;
there, in that future, too abstract
for us to have a right to eye it

together—which just proves that it
already has arrived, for we're
apart—so in this too concrete
future of ours that's clearly here,

and probably for long—a roar
of blizzard plus primeval howls
shrunk to words' status underscore
a wish to play at keeping house—

there, in that future, one thing will
console your heart or give some solace
—to that extent my voice is still
prophetic—to your mind, like stories

narrated by Scheherazade,
with the distinction that my fear
is rather posthumous while what
was hers dealt with plain death—so, dear,

let me now have, wagging my so-
called tongue of native asps, a try at
consoling you, while on the snow
their shadows make good Euclid triumph.

.　　.　　.

When you recall me in that land
on such and such day, month, Lord's summer,
beyond all seas and firmament
whose total I would hate to sum up

for it's much more than could be spent
by us, and having armed your pupil
with the said tear, take up a pen
and on a sheet of plain white paper

draw, like a buttress to the sky,
a perpendicular between two
quite humble points, for that's what, I
suppose, we will be shriveled into

by Time (who knows, by then we, both
invisible, may feel elation
at being famed at least as points)—
at any rate, a separation

is but a firmly drawn straight line,
and a date-hungry pair of lovers—
by that I mean your gaze and mine—
will climb up to the spheres where hovers

that perpendicular's sharp pin
(for, short of realms where angels wrangle,
there is no cave to hide them in);
and isn't that a fine triangle!

Let's analyze this figure which
would at another season force us
to wake up sweating, grab a switch,
tuck heads below the open faucet

to keep the mind from getting scorched
by horrid, all-consuming malice;
and if we both were saved from such
a fate and didn't drink this chalice

of jealousy, dark omens, lies,
spoils, comets, opiates, pure menace,
it was in order to entice
us in the end to sketch its semblance.

Let's analyze it. Time's upon
us: the embrace's stifling blindness
was in itself a pledge of an
invisibility that binds us

in separations: hid within
each other, we dodged space; our shoulder
blades played its borderline; I mean,
it couldn't hurdle them; small wonder

then that it smites a hundredfold
the treacherous—take pen and paper
(the latter symbolizing old
space here) and having found the proper

proportion—one may fancy all
space, since the world has limits, guarded
if not by some cherubic corps,
then by quite stratospheric ardent

emotion—having found it,
the straight line's (cutting us asunder)
proportion to the spacelike sheet,
and having spread an atlas under

this draft, break it into degrees,
then sacrifice that line to rigors
of their dense grid; and you will see
how life will overwhelm love's figures.

So let's presume the line's true length
is known to us, that it would feature
the given couple's lot, or, let
us be more accurate, a picture

of realms in which the two won't meet;
and if this estimate may enter
as a true one (alas, it may),
then, raised from this line's very center,

the perpendicular is but
a sum of these two piercing glances,
and due to their sheer force and jut,
the apex of our figure dances

within the stratosphere: it's quite
unlikely that their sum may ever
pitch higher, for each one's a side
of this isosceles endeavor.

Thus beams of two searchlights that prowl
advertently a hostile chaos
discover their elusive goal
crisscrossing far beyond night clouds;

the goal, though, isn't a target for
the soldiers: in its core, it's rather
a mirror where some would stare
while scared of looking at each other

directly; therefore, who else
but me, one side of that great figure,
should tackle for you this inverse
trite theorem where life, beleaguer-

ing our eyes with all kinds of
its certified scarecrows, gets formal
and tells us to determine now
our angle—in plain words: a corner.

That's what's been *given*. In a guise
of years, of all landscapes, or better
still, in a form of otherwise
unpalpable pervasive matter.

That's our meeting place. A spot
in clouds. A seraphic grotto.
A pergola in spheres. A sort
of corner—a good one, I ought to

admit: there is no one to seize
us hiding in those fleecy orchards
owned solely by our eyes:
the ultimate attempt to purchase.

In years that lie ahead—at best
we'll meet right after death—we'll surely
try to domesticate this nest
by lining it, in night shifts, duly,

with all the trash of lonely thoughts,
of things unsaid—with all that litter
which we'd pile up in our slots
so that it will, sooner or later,

acquire mass enough to strut,
a semblance of material substance,
a status of a star and that
intrinsic light which hardly suffers

because of clouds: for Euclid sees
to it himself that spheres encourage
two corners, alias angles, with
a third one. And it makes a marriage.

That's our *given* then. For quite
a while. Until we hit the coffin.
Apart. Out of each other's sight.
Though from that apex we'll be often

observed; perhaps too often: day
and night, and under either ceiling,
Eastern or Western. And we may
get quite enslaved by that all-seeing

eye finally. No matter how
securely real things imprison
the dark, put this bright pupil now
into your charts, before the risen

all-seeing eye has made out some
of our words! So separation
means our three sharp angles' sum,
while all its agony (let's ration-

alize) is just a product of
their mutual gravitation, which is
far stronger than the other stuff's,
than that of earth's with all its riches.

                    .    .    .

Scholastics, you may utter. Yes,
scholastics, and a shameless hide-and-
seek game with grief. But look and guess:
a star above the sea horizon,

what is it but (permit this turn
so that you won't detect a surplus
of elevated style) a corn
rubbed by the light on space's surface?

Scholastics? Almost. Just as well.
God knows. Take any for a spastic
consent. For after all, pray tell,
what in this world is not scholastic?

God knows. It's rather late. I sink
deep into drowsiness. And winter's
demise in windows builds no link
to springtime. Like the cause that withers

bereft of its effect. My mind
swarms with odd numbers, angles, corners,
with your or my palm stroking my
or your cheekbone.
                        When you recall me
someday, recall the wrapped in black
night shrouds, hanging high, somewhere
out there, over Skagerrak,
accompanied by somewhat gayer

clear planets, shimmering with mist-
like distant light, a lone, name-lacking
star that in fact does not exist.
But this is what the Art of loving

or that of living's all about:
to see that flesh that nature hasn't,
and where the vacuum is, scout
for treasures and for omnipresent

winged female-breasted lions or
dark idols, rather small but able,
great eagles that foretell the score.
Much simpler, then, than all this labor

of making up these things, of spin-
ning promptly from both earth and water
their epidermis and so on,
to set in space a mere iota.

Point out into the midnight haze.
In which direction? Well, in either.
What matters is not what life has,
but just one's faith in what should be there.

Point your sharp finger in the dark:
there, like an alto left to harden
in highest pitch, should be a star;
and if it isn't up there, pardon

long similes, their worn supply;
like roosters that have missed their hour,
the mind, diminished badly by
our parting, simply tries to soar.

*1970 / Translated by David Rigsbee with the author*

# The End of a Beautiful Era

Since the stern art of poetry calls for words, I, morose,
deaf, and balding ambassador of a more or less
    insignificant nation that's stuck in this super
power, wishing to spare my old brain,
put on clothes—all by myself—and head for the main
    street: for the evening paper.

Wind disperses the foliage. The dimness of old bulbs in these
sorry quarters, whose motto's "The mirror will please,"
    gives a sense of abundance supported by puddles.
Even thieves here steal apples by scratching the amalgam first.
Yet the feeling one gets, looking at his reflection—this feeling I've
                                  lost.
    That's what really puzzles.

Everything in these parts is geared for winter: long dreams,
prison walls, overcoats, bridal dresses of whiteness that seems
    snowlike. Drinks. Kinds of dirt in proportion to soaps in dark
                                    corners.
Sparrow vests, second hand of the watch round your wrist,
puritanical mores, underwear. And, tucked in the violinists'
    palms, brown wooden hand-warmers.

This whole realm is just static. Imagining the output of lead
and cast iron, and shaking your stupefied head,
    you recall bayonets, Cossack whips of old power.
But the eagles land like good lodestones on the scraps.
Even wicker chairs here are built mostly with bolts and with nuts,
    one is bound to discover.

Only fish in the sea seem to know freedom's price.
But their muteness compels us to sit and devise
    cashier booths of our own. And space rises like some bill of
                                     fare.

Time's invented by death. In its search for the objects, it deals
with raw vegetables first. And that's why cocks are keen on the
                                               bells
    chiming deafly somewhere.

To exist in the Era of Deeds and to stay elevated, alert
ain't so easy, alas. Having raised a long skirt,
    you will find not new wonders but what you expected.
And it's not that they play Lobachevsky's ideas by ear,
but the widened horizons should narrow somewhere, and here—
    here's the end of perspective.

Either old Europe's map has been swiped by the gents in plain
                                               clothes,
or the famous five-sixths of remaining landmass has just lost
    its infamous colleague, or a fairy casts spells over shabby
me, who knows—but I cannot escape from this place;
I pour wine for myself (service here's a disgrace),
    sip, and rub my old tabby.

Does my brain earn a slug, as a spot where an error occurred
earns a good pointing finger? Or should I hit waterways, sort
    of like Christ? Anyway, in these laudable quarters,
eyes dumfounded by ice and by booze
will reproach you alike for whatever you choose:
    traceless rails, traceless waters.

Now let's see what they say in the papers about lawsuits.
"The condemned has been dealt with." Having read this, a denizen
                                               puts
    on his metal-rimmed glasses that help to relate it
to a man lying flat, his face down, by the wall;
though he isn't asleep. For the dreams do appall
    skulls that are perforated.

The keen-sightedness of our era takes root in the times
which were short, in their blindness, of drawing clear lines
    twixt those fallen from cradles and fallen from saddles.
There are plenty of saucers, but no one to turn tables with
to subject you, poor Rurik, to a sensible quiz;
    that's what really saddens.

The keen-sightedness of our days is the sort that befits the dead end
whose concrete begs for spittle and not for a witty comment.
　　Wake up a dinosaur, not a prince, to recite you the moral!
Birds have feathers for penning last words, though it's better to ask.
For the innocent head there is nothing in store but an ax
　　and the evergreen laurel.

*Leningrad, 1969  /  Translated by David Rigsbee with the author*

# Lithuanian Divertissement

[*For Tomas Venclova*]

## I / Introduction

A modest little country by the sea.
It has its snow, an airport, telephones,
its Jews. A tyrant's brownstone villa.
A statue of a bard is there as well,
who once compared his country to his girlfriend.

The simile displayed, if not good taste,
sound geography: for here the southerners
make Saturday the day to go up north,
from whence, a little drunk, on foot,
they have been known to stray into the West—
a good theme for a sketch. Here distances
are well designed to suit hermaphrodites.

Noonday in springtime. Puddles, banked-up clouds,
stout, countless angels on the gables
of countless churches. Here a man
becomes a victim of a jostling crowd,
or a detail of the homemade baroque.

## II / Liejyklos

To be born a century ago
and over the down bedding, airing,
through a window see a garden grow
and Catherine's crosses, twin domes soaring;
be embarrassed for Mother, hiccup
when the brandished lorgnettes scrutinize
and push a cart with rubbish heaped up
along the ghetto's yellow alleys,
sigh, tucked in bed from head to toe,
for Polish ladies, for example;

and hang around to face the foe
and fall in Poland somewhere, trampled—
for Faith, Tsar, Homeland, or if not,
then shape Jews' ringlets into sideburns
and off, on to the New World like a shot,
puking in waves as the engine churns.

### III / Café Neringa

Time departs in Vilnius through a café door
accompanied by sounds of clinking forks and spoons,
while Space screws up its eyes from booze the night before
and stares at Time's slowly retreating spine.

A crimson circle, with its far side off,
now hangs moored in utter stillness over roof tiles
and the Adam's apple sharpens, quite as if
the whole face had shrunk to its sheer profile.

Obeying commands like Aladdin's lamp,
a waitress decked out in a cambric halter
saunters about with legs recently clamped
around the neck of a local footballer.

### IV / Escutcheon

St. George, that old dragon slayer,
spear long lost in allegory's glare,
has kept in safety up till now
his sword and steed, and every place
in Lithuania pursues, steadfast,
his aim unheeded by the crowd.

Who now has he, sword clenched in hand,
resolved on taking? What he hounds,
a well-placed coat of arms blots out.
Who can it be? Gentile? Saracen?
The whole world, perhaps? If that's so, then
Vytautas knew well what he was about.

## V / *Amicum-philosophum de melancholia, mania et plica polonica*

Sleeplessness. Part of a woman. A glass
replete with reptiles all straining to get out.
The day's long madness has drained across
the cerebellum into the occiput,
forming a pool; one movement and the slush
will feel as if someone, in that icy blot,
has dipped a sharpened quill that, after a pause,
deliberately traces the verb "hate"
in oscillating scribbles to reverse
the brain-wave pattern. Something lipsticked stuffs
the ear with lacerating lengthy words,
like running fingers through a hairdo stiff
with lice. Alone and naked in your sack,
you lie there, fallen from the Zodiac.

## VI / *Palanga*

Only the sea has power to peer en face
at the sky; and a traveler in the dunes
lowers his eyes and sips at his metal flask
like a king in exile, with no psalm-like tunes.

His house ransacked, flocks driven to foreign land.
Son hidden by shepherds inside a cave.
And before him lies just a hem of sand
but his faith's not enough for a walk on waves.

## VII / *The Dominicans*

Turn off the thoroughfare, then into
a half-blind street, and once inside
the church, which at this hour is empty,
sit on a bench, adjust your sight,
and, afterward, in God's whorled ear,
closed to the clash of day's discord,
whisper four syllables, soft and clear:
    Forgive me, Lord.

*1971 / Translated by Alan Myers*

# *On Love*

Twice I woke up tonight and wandered to
the window. And the lights down on the street,
like pale omission points, tried to complete
the fragment of a sentence spoken through
sleep, but diminished into darkness, too.

I'd dreamt that you were pregnant, and in spite
of having lived so many years apart
I still felt guilty and my heartened palm
caressed your belly as, by the bedside,
it fumbled for my trousers and the light-

switch on the wall. And with the bulb turned on
I knew that I was leaving you alone
there, in the darkness, in the dream, where calmly
you waited till I might return,
not trying to reproach or scold me

for the unnatural hiatus. For
darkness restores what light cannot repair.
There we are married, blest, we make once more
the two-backed beast and children are the fair
excuse of what we're naked for.

Some future night you will appear again.
You'll come to me, worn out and thin now, after
things in between, and I'll see son or daughter
not named as yet. This time I will restrain
my hand from groping for the switch, afraid

and feeling that I have no right
to leave you both like shadows by that sever-
ing fence of days that bar your sight,
voiceless, negated by the real light
that keeps me unattainable forever.

*1971  /  Translated by Daniel Weissbort with the author*

# I Sit by the Window

[ *For Lev Loseff* ]

I said fate plays a game without a score,
and who needs fish if you've got caviar?
The triumph of the Gothic style would come to pass
and turn you on—no need for coke, or grass.
    I sit by the window. Outside, an aspen.
    When I loved, I loved deeply. It wasn't often.

I said the forest's only part of a tree.
Who needs the whole girl if you've got her knee?
Sick of the dust raised by the modern era,
the Russian eye would rest on an Estonian spire.
    I sit by the window. The dishes are done.
    I was happy here. But I won't be again.

I wrote: The bulb looks at the floor in fear,
and love, as an act, lacks a verb; the zer-
o Euclid thought the vanishing point became
wasn't math—it was the nothingness of Time.
    I sit by the window. And while I sit
    my youth comes back. Sometimes I'd smile. Or spit.

I said that the leaf may destroy the bud;
what's fertile falls in fallow soil—a dud;
that on the flat field, the unshadowed plain
nature spills the seeds of trees in vain.
    I sit by the window. Hands lock my knees.
    My heavy shadow's my squat company.

My song was out of tune, my voice was cracked,
but at least no chorus can ever sing it back.
That talk like this reaps no reward bewilders
no one—no one's legs rest on my shoulders.
    I sit by the window in the dark. Like an express,
    the waves behind the wavelike curtain crash.

A loyal subject of these second-rate years,
I proudly admit that my finest ideas
are second-rate, and may the future take them
as trophies of my struggle against suffocation.
    I sit in the dark. And it would be hard to figure out
    which is worse: the dark inside, or the darkness out.

*1971 / Translated by Howard Moss*

# Nature Morte

*Verrà la morte e avrà i tuoi occhi.* —Cesare Pavese

### I

People and things crowd in.
Eyes can be bruised and hurt
by people as well as things.
Better to live in the dark.

I sit on a wooden bench
watching the passers-by—
sometimes whole families.
I am fed up with the light.

This is a winter month.
First on the calendar.
I shall begin to speak
when I'm fed up with the dark.

### II

It's time. I shall now begin.
It makes no difference with what.
Open mouth. It is better to speak,
although I can also be mute.

What then shall I talk about?
Shall I talk about nothingness?
Shall I talk about days, or nights?
Or people? No, only things,

since people will surely die.
All of them. As I shall.
All talk is a barren trade.
A writing on the wind's wall.

### III

My blood is very cold—
its cold is more withering

than iced-to-the-bottom streams.
People are not my thing.

I hate the look of them.
Grafted to life's great tree,
each face is firmly stuck
and cannot be torn free.

Something the mind abhors
shows in each face and form.
Something like flattery
of persons quite unknown.

IV

Things are more pleasant. Their
outsides are neither good
nor evil. And their insides
reveal neither good nor bad.

The core of things is dry rot.
Dust. A wood borer. And
brittle moth-wings. Thin walls.
Uncomfortable to the hand.

Dust. When you switch lights on,
there's nothing but dust to see.
That's true even if the thing
is sealed up hermetically.

V

This ancient cabinet—
outside as well as in—
strangely reminds me of
Paris's Notre Dame.

Everything's dark within
it. Dust mop or bishop's stole
can't touch the dust of things.
Things themselves, as a rule,

don't try to purge or tame
the dust of their own insides.

Dust is the flesh of time.
Time's very flesh and blood.

## VI

Lately I often sleep
during the daytime. My
death, it would seem, is now
trying and testing me,

placing a mirror close
to my still-breathing lips,
seeing if I can stand
non-being in daylight.

I do not move. These two
thighs are like blocks of ice.
Branched veins show blue against
skin that is marble white.

## VII

Summing their angles up
as a surprise to us,
things drop away from man's
world—a world made with words.

Things do not move, or stand.
That's our delirium.
Each thing's a space, beyond
which there can be no thing.

A thing can be battered, burned,
gutted, and broken up.
Thrown out. And yet the thing
never will yell, "Oh, fuck!"

## VIII

A tree. Its shadow, and
earth, pierced by clinging roots.
Interlaced monograms.
Clay and a clutch of rocks.

Roots interweave and blend.
Stones have their private mass

[ 45 ]

which frees them from the bond
of normal rootedness.

This stone is fixed. One can't
move it, or heave it out.
Tree shadows catch a man,
like a fish, in their net.

IX

A thing. Its brown color. Its
blurry outline. Twilight.
Now there is nothing left.
Only a *nature morte*.

Death will come and will find
a body whose silent peace
will reflect death's approach
like any woman's face.

Scythe, skull, and skeleton—
an absurd pack of lies.
Rather: "Death, when it comes,
will have your own two eyes."

X

Mary now speaks to Christ:
"Are you my son?—or God?
You are nailed to the cross.
Where lies my homeward road?

Can I pass through my gate
not having understood:
Are you dead?—or alive?
Are you my son?—or God?"

Christ speaks to her in turn:
"Whether dead or alive,
woman, it's all the same—
son or God, I am thine."

*1971  /  Translated by George L. Kline*

# December 24, 1971

[ *For V.S.* ]

When it's Christmas we're all of us magi.
At the grocers' all slipping and pushing.
Where a tin of halvah, coffee-flavored,
is the cause of a human assault-wave
by a crowd heavy-laden with parcels:
each one his own king, his own camel.

Nylon bags, carrier bags, paper cones,
caps and neckties all twisted up sideways.
Reek of vodka and resin and cod,
orange mandarins, cinnamon, apples.
Floods of faces, no sign of a pathway
toward Bethlehem, shut off by blizzard.

And the bearers of moderate gifts
leap on buses and jam all the doorways,
disappear into courtyards that gape,
though they know that there's nothing inside there:
not a beast, not a crib, nor yet her,
round whose head gleams a nimbus of gold.

Emptiness. But the mere thought of that
brings forth lights as if out of nowhere.
Herod reigns but the stronger he is,
the more sure, the more certain the wonder.
In the constancy of this relation
is the basic mechanics of Christmas.

That's what they celebrate everywhere,
for its coming push tables together.
No demand for a star for a while,
but a sort of good will touched with grace
can be seen in all men from afar,
and the shepherds have kindled their fires.

Snow is falling: not smoking but sounding
chimney pots on the roof, every face like a stain.
Herod drinks. Every wife hides her child.
He who comes is a mystery: features
are not known beforehand, men's hearts may
not be quick to distinguish the stranger.

But when drafts through the doorway disperse
the thick mist of the hours of darkness
and a shape in a shawl stands revealed,
both a newborn and Spirit that's Holy
in your self you discover; you stare
skyward, and it's right there:
                                        a star.

*1972  /  Translated by Alan Myers with the author*

# To a Tyrant

He used to come here till he donned gold braid,
a good topcoat on, self-controlled, stoop-shouldered.
Arresting these café habitués—
he started snuffing out world culture somewhat later—
seemed sweet revenge (on Time, that is, not them)
for all the lack of cash, the sneers and insults,
the lousy coffee, boredom, and the battles
at vingt-et-un he lost time and again.

And Time has had to stomach that revenge.
The place is now quite crowded; bursts of laughter,
records boom out. But just before you sit
you seem to feel an urge to turn your head around.
Plastic and chrome are everywhere—not right;
the pastries have an aftertaste of bromide.
Sometimes before the place shuts down he'll enter
straight from a theater, anonymous, no fuss.

When he comes in, the lot of them stand up.
Some out of duty, the rest in unfeigned joy.
Limp-wristed, with a languid sweep of palm,
he gives the evening back its cozy feel.
He drinks his coffee—better, nowadays—
and bites a roll, while perching on his chair,
so tasty that the very dead would cry
"Oh, yes!" if only they could rise and be there.

*1972  /  Translated by Alan Myers*

# The Funeral of Bobò

---

### I

Bobò is dead, but don't take off your hat.
No gesture we could make will help us bear it.
Why mount a butterfly upon the spit
of the Admiralty tower? We'd only tear it.

On every side, no matter where you glance,
are squares of windows. As for "What happened?"—well,
open an empty can by way of answer,
and say, "Just that, as near as one can tell."

Bobò is dead. Wednesday is almost over.
On streets which offer you no place to go,
such whiteness lies. Only the night river,
with its black water, does not wear the snow.

### II

Bobò is dead; there's sadness in this line.
O window squares, O arches' semicircles,
and such fierce frost that if one's to be slain,
let blazing firearms do the dirty work.

Farewell, Bobò, my beautiful and sweet.
These teardrops dot the page like holes in cheese.
We are too weak to follow you, and yet
to take a stand exceeds our energies.

Your image, as I here and now predict,
whether in crackling cold or waves of heat,
shall never dwindle—quite the reverse, in fact—
in Rossi's matchless, long, and tapering street.

### III

Bobò is dead. Something I might convey
slips from my grasp, as bath soap sometimes does.

Today, within a dream, I seemed to lie
upon my bed. And there, in fact, I was.

Tear off a page, but read the date aright:
it's with a zero that our woes commence.
Without her, dreams suggest the waking state,
and squares of air push through the window vents.

Bobò is dead. One feels an impulse, with
half-parted lips, to murmur "Why? What for?"
It's emptiness, no doubt, which follows death.
That's likelier than hell—and worse, what's more.

IV

You were all things, Bobò. But your decease
has changed you. You are nothing; you are not;
or, rather, you are a clot of emptiness—
which also, come to think of it, is a lot.

Bobò is dead. To these round eyes, the view
of the bare horizon line is like a knife.
But neither Kiki nor Zazà, Bobò,
will ever take your place. Not on your life.

Now Thursday. I believe in emptiness.
There, it's like hell, but shittier, I've heard.
And the new Dante, pregnant with his message,
bends to the empty page and writes a word.

*1972 / Translated by Richard Wilbur*

# Letters to a Roman Friend

### I

Now it's windy and the waves are running crisscross.
    Soon it will be fall, and nature's face will alter.
Shifts in these bright colors stir me more profoundly,
    Postumus, than changes in my lady's wardrobe.

To a certain point a girl can satisfy you—
    if you don't go farther than her knees or elbows.
But how much more joyous the unbodied beauty
    of an autumn wood: no kisses, no betrayals!

### II

Postumus, I'm sending books, I hope you'll like them.
    How's Imperial Rome?—A soft bed, hard to sleep on?
How fares Caesar? What's he up to? Still intriguing?
    —Still intriguing, probably, and overeating.

In the garden where I sit a torch is burning.
    I'm alone—no lady, servant, or acquaintance.
Not the humble of this world, nor yet its mighty—
    nothing but the buzzing of an insect chorus.

### III

In this graveyard lies a merchant out of Asia.
    He was clever, able, yet he passed unnoticed.
He died suddenly, of fever. Not to this end
    did he sail here, but to make a profit.

Underneath unpolished quartz there lies beside him
    an Imperial legionnaire, renowned in battle.
Target of a thousand thrusts, he lived till eighty.
    Rules here, Postumus, are proved by their exceptions.

### IV

Birds aren't very bright, my Postumus, that's certain;
    but there's misery enough even for bird-brains.

If one's fated to be born in Caesar's Empire
    let him live aloof, provincial, by the seashore.

One who lives remote from snowstorms, and from Caesar,
    has no need to hurry, flatter, play the coward.
You may say that local governors are vultures.
    I, for one, prefer a vulture to a vampire.

V

I'm prepared, hetaera, to wait out this downpour
    in your company. But let us have no haggling.
Snatching silver coins from this, my covering body,
    is like ripping shingles from the roof above you.

This roof's sprung a leak, you say? But where's the puddle?
    I have never left a wet spot; no, not ever.
Better go and find yourself a proper husband:
    he will do it to your sheets and pay the laundry.

VI

Here we've spent—I swear it—more than half our lifetimes.
    As a slave—now white-haired—told me near the tavern:
"When we look around us, all we see is ruins."
    A barbarian perspective, though a true one.

I'm back from the mountains carrying fresh wildflowers.
    I'll get out a jug and fill it with cool water.
What's the latest from that Libya or wherever?
    Are we still engaged in all that desert fighting?

VII

Friend, do you remember our Proconsul's sister—
    rather skinny, though her calves were heavy?
You had slept with her . . . Well, she became a priestess—
    priestess, Postumus, with gods for her companions.

Come and visit me, and we'll drink wine together.
    Plums are ripe and bread is good. You'll bring the gossip.
I shall make your couch up in the star-swept garden
    and teach you to name our local constellations.

## VIII

Soon, dear Postumus, your friend who loves addition
    will pay off his debt, his old debt, to subtraction.
Take my savings, then, from underneath my pillow—
    though not much, they'll pay the cost of my interment.

Post on your black mare to the House of Hetaeras
    hard against the wall of our provincial city.
Give each girl the sum for which she once embraced me:
    let them mourn me for the same amount of money.

## IX

Dark green laurels on the verge of trembling.
    Doors ajar. The windowpane is dusty.
Idle chairs and the abandoned sofa.
    Linen blinded by the sun of noonday.

Pontus drones past a black fence of pine trees.
    Someone's boat braves gusts out by the promontory.
On the garden bench a book of Pliny rustles.
    Thrushes chirp within the hairdo of the cypress.

*1972 / Translated by George L. Kline*

# *Nunc Dimittis*

When Mary first came to present the Christ Child
to God in His temple, she found—of those few
who fasted and prayed there, departing not from it—
    devout Simeon and the prophetess Anna.

The holy man took the Babe up in his arms.
The three of them, lost in the grayness of dawn,
now stood like a small shifting frame that surrounded
    the Child in the palpable dark of the temple.

The temple enclosed them in forests of stone.
Its lofty vaults stooped as though trying to cloak
the prophetess Anna, and Simeon, and Mary—
    to hide them from men and to hide them from heaven.

And only a chance ray of light struck the hair
of that sleeping Infant, who stirred but as yet
was conscious of nothing and blew drowsy bubbles;
    old Simeon's arms held him like a stout cradle.

It had been revealed to this upright old man
that he would not die until his eyes had seen
the Son of the Lord. And it thus came to pass. And
    he said: "Now, O Lord, lettest thou thy poor servant,

according to thy holy word, leave in peace,
for mine eyes have witnessed thine offspring: he is
thy continuation and also the source of
    thy Light for idolatrous tribes, and the glory

of Israel as well." Then old Simeon paused.
The silence, regaining the temple's clear space,
oozed from all its corners and almost engulfed them,
    and only his echoing words grazed the rafters,

to spin for a moment, with faint rustling sounds,
high over their heads in the tall temple's vaults,
akin to a bird that can soar, yet that cannot
      return to the earth, even if it should want to.

A strangeness engulfed them. The silence now seemed
as strange as the words of old Simeon's speech.
And Mary, confused and bewildered, said nothing—
      so strange had his words been. He added, while turning

directly to Mary: "Behold, in this Child,
now close to thy breast, is concealed the great fall
of many, the great elevation of others,
      a subject of strife and a source of dissension,

and that very steel which will torture his flesh
shall pierce through thine own soul as well. And that wound
will show to thee, Mary, as in a new vision
      what lies hidden, deep in the hearts of all people."

He ended and moved toward the temple's great door.
Old Anna, bent down with the weight of her years,
and Mary, now stooping, gazed after him, silent.
      He moved and grew smaller, in size and in meaning,

to these two frail women who stood in the gloom.
As though driven on by the force of their looks,
he strode through the cold empty space of the temple
      and moved toward the whitening blur of the doorway.

The stride of his old legs was steady and firm.
When Anna's voice sounded behind him, he slowed
his step for a moment. But she was not calling
      to him; she had started to bless God and praise Him.

The door came still closer. The wind stirred his robe
and fanned at his forehead; the roar of the street,
exploding in life by the door of the temple,
      beat stubbornly into old Simeon's hearing.

He went forth to die. It was not the loud din
of streets that he faced when he flung the door wide,
but rather the deaf-and-dumb fields of death's kingdom.
    He strode through a space that was no longer solid.

The rustle of time ebbed away in his ears.
And Simeon's soul held the form of the Child—
its feathery crown now enveloped in glory—
    aloft, like a torch, pressing back the black shadows,

to light up the path that leads into death's realm,
where never before until this present hour
had any man managed to lighten his pathway.
    The old man's torch glowed and the pathway grew wider.

*February 16, 1972 / Translated by George L. Kline*

# Odysseus to Telemachus

My dear Telemachus,
                          The Trojan War
is over now; I don't recall who won it.
The Greeks, no doubt, for only they would leave
so many dead so far from their own homeland.
But still, my homeward way has proved too long.
While we were wasting time there, old Poseidon,
it almost seems, stretched and extended space.

I don't know where I am or what this place
can be. It would appear some filthy island,
with bushes, buildings, and great grunting pigs.
A garden choked with weeds; some queen or other.
Grass and huge stones . . . Telemachus, my son!
To a wanderer the faces of all islands
resemble one another. And the mind
trips, numbering waves; eyes, sore from sea horizons,
run; and the flesh of water stuffs the ears.
I can't remember how the war came out;
even how old you are—I can't remember.

Grow up, then, my Telemachus, grow strong.
Only the gods know if we'll see each other
again. You've long since ceased to be that babe
before whom I reined in the plowing bullocks.
Had it not been for Palamedes' trick
we two would still be living in one household.
But maybe he was right; away from me
you are quite safe from all Oedipal passions,
and your dreams, my Telemachus, are blameless.

*1972  /  Translated by George L. Kline*

# A Part of Speech

An autumn evening in the modest square
of a small town proud to have made the atlas
(some frenzy drove that poor mapmaker witless,
or else he had the daughter of the mayor).

Here Space appears unnerved by its own feats
and glad to drop the burden of its greatness—
to shrink to the dimensions of Main Street;
and Time, chilled to its bone, stares at the clockface
above the general store, whose crowded shelves
hold every item that this world produces,
from fancy amateur stargazers' tel-
escopes to common pins for common uses.

A movie theater, a few saloons,
around the bend a café with drawn shutters,
a red-brick bank topped with spread-eagle plumes,
a church, whose net—to fish for men—now flutters
unfilled, and which would be paid little heed,
except that it stands next to the post office.
And if parishioners should cease to breed,
the pastor would start christening their autos.

Grasshoppers, in the silence, run amok.
By 6 p.m. the city streets are empty,
unpeopled as if by a nuclear strike.
Just surfacing, the moon swims to the center
of this black window square, like some Eccles-
iastes, glowering; while on the lonely
highway, from time to time, a Buick beams
its blinding headlights at the Unknown Soldier.

The dreams you dream are not of girls half nude
but of your name on an arriving letter.

A morning milkman, seeing milk that's soured,
will be the first to guess that you have died here.
Here you can live, ignoring calendars,
gulp Bromo, never leave the house; just settle
and stare at your reflection in the glass,
as streetlamps stare at theirs in shrinking puddles.

*1972 / Translated by George L. Kline*

# *1972*

[ *For V.G.* ]

Birds don't fly through my skylight nowadays.
A girl, like a beast, guards her noble place.
If I chance to slip up on nobody's
cherrystone, I don't fall, since friction's
increased with the failed velocity.
The heart, like a squirrel in brushwood, is tossing up
ribs. And the throat celebrates the atrocity
of old age; lists its huge afflictions.

Aging! Hail to thee, senility.
Blood flows as slowly as chilly tea.
Limbs, former pride of the whole vicinity,
hurt my vision. And rather gingerly
I stuff the threatened fifth field of feeling—
when taking my shoes off—with cotton fillings.
The man with a spade is now a fitting
sight, as the knife said to the injury.

Rightly so! The body repents its proclivities.
All these singing, weeping, and snarled activities.
As for my dental cave, its cavities
rival old Troy on a rainy day.
Joints cracking loud and breath like a sewer,
I foul the mirror. It's premature
to talk of the shroud. But you may be sure,
those who'll carry you out besiege the doorway.

Well met, then, joyful, young, unfamiliar
tribe! Buzzing around my jugular,
time has discovered at last its singular
sweetmeat in my resilient cranium.
Thoughts are uncombed and a pogrom scours
my scalp. Like Ivan's queen in her tower,
all fibers sense the dark breathing powers;
I scramble the bedding but try to carry on.

Frightening! That's it, exactly, frightening.
Even when all the wheels of the train keep thundering
below your waistline, there is no faltering
for the flight of fancy. Like the amnesia-
stricken gaze of a graduate with his freckled face,
who confuses a bra with a pair of spectacles,
pain is weak-eyed and death in its speckledness
looks like the vague outlines of Asia.

All that I could have lost has been totally
lost. But also I've gained approximately
all those things I was in for. Oddly
enough, even a cuckoo's crooning in darkness
moves me little—let life be vilified
by her plangent notes, or affirmed and verified.
Aging is growth of a new but a very fine
hearing that only to silence hearkens.

Aging! The body reeks of mortality,
that is, of what's useless to life. From my metallic brow
the radiance cast over this locality
vanishes. And at noon a black searchlight harbors
in my sunken pupils. The strength, the gallantry
are stolen away from my muscles cowardly.
But I do not search for a gallows tree:
shameful to take on the Lord's own labors.

The point is, most likely, pure cowardice.
Fear. The technical side of the enterprise.
It's the imminent necrosis's menacing old device:
any erosion begins with willing,
the minimum of which is the heart, the basis
of stasis. Or so I was told while in that oasis
of school. Remove, dear chums, your faces!
Let me out into open valley!

I was much like the rest, that is, lived a similar
life. Would appear in halls with wisteria.
Drank a fair bit. Dragged my fool under the skin of a . . .
Used to take what was given. The soul didn't hanker for
what wasn't hers. Had a stable ground,
fashioned a lever. Or would produce a sound

from my hollow pipe fitting the space around.
What should I say before curtain fall?

Listen, my boon brethren and my enemies!
What I've done, I've done not for fame or memories
in this era of radio waves and cinemas,
but for the sake of my native tongue and letters.
For which sort of devotion, of a zealous bent
("Heal thyself, doctor," as the saying went),
denied a chalice at the feast of the fatherland,
now I stand in a strange place. The name hardly matters.

It's windy, dank, dark. And it's windy. Hence
midnight flings branches and leaves onto fence
and roof tiles. Now I can state with confidence:
here I'll live out my days, losing gradually
hair, teeth, consonants, verbs, and suffixes,
with this hat of mine ladling the ocean surface, as
with Prince Igor's helmet, just to reduce its size,
munching raw fish, behaving naturally.

Aging! The time of success. Of acknowledging
truth. Of its sullied linen. Of banishment. Of discouraging
pain. As for the latter, I neither nourish it
nor dismiss it. If it gets hard, annoying,
I'll yell out: self-restraint is just dumb and morbid.
As for now, I can take a bit more of it.
If an ember still glows inside this monolith,
it's not reason, just blood that keeps circling, going.

This song isn't the desperate howl of deep distress.
It's the species' trip back to the wilderness.
It's, more aptly, the first cry of speechlessness,
whose domain could be thought just a total feat
of sounds voiced by a once scarlet and
wet—now hardening into a moribund
more or less matter—strong vocal vent.
Change for the better. Or that's my view of it.

Lo! that's the point of my speech, I'm proud of making it:
of the body's conversion into a naked thing,
object—against a vast, vacant, and

empty space, be it lit up by so much fire.
Still, change for the best, since fright, horror, shudders
are alien to objects. So little puddles
won't be found under objects like under others,
even when your small object is to expire.

Just like Theseus out from the lair in the Minos ring,
coming up for air with the pelt of that menacing
beast, it's not a horizon I see but a minus sign
on my previous life. This line is clearly
keener than a hero's sword, and shorn off by its cutting blade
the dearest part. Thus they take away a costly blend
from the sober man, and salt from what's bland.
I feel like crying. But it's pointless, really.

Beat, then, the drum of your faith in shears
where the fate of all matter these days inheres.
Only a good-sized loss in the local spheres
makes a mortal equal to God. (This arching
observation is worthy of real emphasis
even in the view of amorous nakedness.)
Beat, see how much sticks and drums can take of this,
marching along while your shadow's marching.

*1972 / Translated by Alan Myers with the author*

# In the Lake District

In those days, in a place where dentists thrive
(their daughters order fancy clothes from London;
their painted forceps hold aloft on signboards
a common and abstracted Wisdom Tooth),
there I—whose mouth held ruins more abject
than any Parthenon—a spy, a spearhead
for some fifth column of a rotting culture
(my cover was a lit. professorship),
was living at a college near the most
renowned of the fresh-water lakes; the function
to which I'd been appointed was to wear out
the patience of the ingenuous local youth.

Whatever I wrote then was incomplete:
my lines expired in strings of dots. Collapsing,
I dropped, still fully dressed, upon my bed.
At night I stared up at the darkened ceiling
until I saw a shooting star, which then,
conforming to the laws of self-combustion,
would flash—before I'd even made a wish—
across my cheek and down onto my pillow.

*Ann Arbor, 1972  /  Translated by George L. Kline*

# The Butterfly

I

Should I say that you're dead?
You touched so brief a fragment
of time. There's much that's sad in
the joke God played.
I scarcely comprehend
the words "you've lived"; the date of
your birth and when you faded
in my cupped hand
are one, and not two dates.
Thus calculated,
your term is, simply stated,
less than a day.

II

It's clear that days for us
are nothings, zeros.
They can't be pinned down near us
to feed our eyes.
Whenever days stand stark
against white borders,
since they possess no bodies
they leave no mark.
They are like you. That is,
each butterfly's small plumage
is one day's shrunken image—
a tenth its size.

III

Should I say that, somehow,
you lack all being?
What, then, are my hands feeling
that's so like you?
Such colors can't be drawn
from nonexistence.

Tell me, at whose insistence
were yours laid on?
Since I'm a mumbling heap
of words, not pigments,
how could your hues be figments
of my conceit?

IV

There are, on your small wings,
black spots and splashes—
like eyes, birds, girls, eyelashes.
But of what things
are you the airy norm?
What bits of faces,
what broken times and places
shine through your form?
As for your *nature morte*s:
do they show dishes
of fruits and flowers, or fishes
displayed on boards?

V

Perhaps a landscape smokes
among your ashes,
and with thick reading glasses
I'll scan its slopes—
its beaches, dancers, nymphs.
Is it as bright as
the day, or dark as night is?
And could one glimpse—
ascending that sky's screen—
some blazing lantern?
And tell me, please, what pattern
inspired this scene?

VI

It seems to me you are
a protean creature,
whose markings mask a feature
of face, or stone, or star.
Who was the jeweler,

brow uncontracted,
who from our world extracted
your miniature—
a world where madness brings
us low, and lower,
where we are things, while you are
the thought of things?

## VII

Why were these lovely shapes
and colors given
for your one day of life in
this land of lakes?
—a land whose dappled mir-
rors have one merit:
reflecting space, they store it.
Such brief existence tore
away your chance
to be captured, delivered,
within cupped hands to quiver—
the hunter's eye entrance.

## VIII

You shun every response—
but not from shyness
or wickedness or slyness,
and not because
you're dead. Dead or alive,
to God's least creature
is given voice for speech, or
for song—a sign
that it has found a way
to bind together,
and stretch life's limits, whether
an hour or day.

## IX

But you lack even this:
the means to utter
a word. Yet, probe the matter;
it's better thus.

You're not in heaven's debt,
on heaven's ledger.
It's not a curse, I pledge you,
that your small weight
and span rob you of tongue.
Sound's burden, too, is grievous.
And you're more speechless,
less fleshed, than time.

X

Living too brief an hour
for fear or trembling,
you spin, motelike, ascending
above this bed of flowers,
beyond the prison space
where past and future
combine to break, or batter,
our lives, and thus
when your path leads you far
to open meadows,
your pulsing wings bring shadows
and shapes to air.

XI

So, too, the sliding pen
which inks a surface
has no sense of the purpose
of any line
or that the whole will end
as an amalgam
of heresy and wisdom;
it therefore trusts the hand
whose silent speech incites
fingers to throbbing—
whose spasm reaps no pollen,
but eases hearts.

XII

Such beauty, set beside
so brief a season,
suggests to our stunned reason

this bleak surmise:
the world was made to hold
no end or *telos*,
and if—as some would tell us—
there is a goal,
it's not ourselves.
No butterfly collector
can trap light or detect where
the darkness dwells.


XIII

Should I bid you farewell
as to a day that's over?
Men's memories may wither,
grow thin, and fall
like hair. The trouble is,
behind their backs are:
not double beds for lovers,
hard sleep, the past,
or days in shrinking files
backstretched—but, rather,
huge clouds, circling together,
of butterflies.


XIV

You're better than No-thing.
That is, you're nearer,
more reachable, and clearer.
Yet you're akin
to nothingness—
like it, you're wholly empty.
And if, in your life's venture,
No-thing takes flesh,
that flesh will die.
Yet while you live you offer
a frail and shifting buffer,
dividing it from me.

*1973  /  Translated by George L. Kline*

# *Torso*

---

If suddenly you walk on grass turned stone
and think its marble handsomer than green,
or see at play a nymph and faun that seem
happier in bronze than in any dream,
let your walking stick fall from your weary hand,
　　　　　you're in The Empire, friend.

Air, fire, water, fauns, naiads, lions
drawn from nature, or bodied in imagination,
everything God ventured and reason grew bored
nourishing have in stone and metal been restored.
This is the end of things. This is, at the road's end,
　　　　　a mirror by which to enter.

Stand in a niche, roll your eyes up, and watch
the ages vanish round the bend, and watch
how moss develops in the statue's groin,
how dust rains on the shoulders—that tan of time.
Someone breaks an arm off, and the head from the shoulders
　　　　　falls with the thud of boulders.

The torso left is a nameless sum of muscle.
In a thousand years a mouse, living in a hole,
with a claw broken off from trying to eke
a life out of granite, will scurry with a squeak
across the road one night and not come back to its burrow
　　　　　at midnight tonight. Or at daybreak tomorrow.

*1973 / Translated by Howard Moss*

# Lagoon

[ *For Brooke and Strobe Talbott* ]

## I

Down in the lobby three elderly women, bored,
take up, with their knitting, the Passion of Our Lord
    as the universe and the tiny realm
of the *pension* Accademia, side by side,
with TV blaring, sail into Christmastide,
    a lookout desk clerk at the helm.

## II

And a nameless lodger, a nobody, boards the boat,
a bottle of grappa concealed in his raincoat
    as he gains his shadowy room, bereaved
of memory, homeland, son, with only the noise
of distant forests to grieve for his former joys,
    if anyone is grieved.

## III

Venetian church bells, teacups, mantel clocks
chime and confound themselves in this stale box
    of assorted lives. The brazen, coiled
octopus-chandelier appears to be licking,
in a triptych mirror, bedsheet and mattress ticking,
    sodden with tears and passion-soiled.

## IV

Blown by night winds, an Adriatic tide
floods the canals, boats rock from side to side,
    moored cradles, and the humble bream,
not ass and oxen, guards the rented bed
where the window blind above your sleeping head
    moves to the sea star's guiding beam.

## V

So this is how we cope, putting out the heat
of grappa with nightstand water, carving the meat
    of flounder instead of Christmas roast,

so that Thy earliest backboned ancestor
might feed and nourish us, O Saviour,
    this winter night on a damp coast.

### VI

A Christmas without snow, tinsel, or tree,
at the edge of a map- and land-corseted sea;
    having scuttled and sunk its scallop shell,
concealing its face while flaunting its backside,
Time rises from the goddess's frothy tide,
    yet changes nothing but clock hand and bell.

### VII

A drowning city, where suddenly the dry
light of reason dissolves in the moisture of the eye;
    its winged lion, which can read and write,
southern kin of northern sphinxes of renown,
won't drop his book and holler, but calmly drown
    in splinters of mirror, splashing light.

### VIII

The gondola knocks against its moorings. Sound
cancels itself, hearing and words are drowned,
    as is that nation where among
forests of hands the tyrant of the State
is voted in, its only candidate,
    and spit goes ice-cold on the tongue.

### IX

So let us place the left paw, sheathing its claws,
in the crook of the arm of the other one, because
    this makes a hammer-and-sickle sign
with which to salute our era and bestow
a mute up-yours-even-unto-the-elbow
    upon the nightmares of our time.

### X

The raincoated figure is settling into place
where Sophia, Constance, Prudence, Faith, and Grace
    lack futures, the only tense that is
is present, where either a goyish or Yiddish kiss
tastes bitter, like the city, where footsteps fade
    invisibly along the colonnade,

trackless and blank as a gondola's passage through
a water surface, smoothing out of view
    the measured wrinkles of its path,
unmarked as a broad "So long!" like the wide piazza's space,
or as a cramped "I love," like the narrow alleyways,
    erased and without aftermath.

Moldings and carvings, palaces and flights
of stairs. Look up: the lion smiles from heights
    of a tower wrapped as in a coat
of wind, unbudged, determined not to yield,
like a rank weed at the edge of a plowed field,
    and girdled round by Time's deep moat.

Night in St. Mark's piazza. A face as creased
as a finger from its fettering ring released,
    biting a nail, is gazing high
into that *nowhere* of pure thought, where sight
is baffled by the bandages of night,
    serene, beyond the naked eye,

where, past all boundaries and all predicates,
black, white, or colorless, vague, volatile states,
    something, some object, comes to mind.
Perhaps a body. In our dim days and few,
the speed of light equals a fleeting view,
    even when blackout robs us blind.

*1973  /  Translated by Anthony Hecht*

[ *For Mikhail Baryshnikov* ]

The classical ballet, let's say, is beauty's keep
whose gentle denizens are moated off from feeling
prosaic things by pits filled up with fiddling,
and drawbridges are hoisted up.

In soft imperial plush you wriggle your backside,
as, thighs aflutter at the speed of shorthand,
a pearl who'll never make your sofa shudder
wings out into the garden in one glide.

We see archfiends in dark-brown leotards
and guardian angels in their tutus flaunting vision;
and then enough applause to rouse from sleep Elysian
Tchaikovsky and the other smarts.

The classical ballet! The art of better days!
When grog went hissing down with kisses ten a penny,
the cabs were tearing by, we sang hey nonny-nonny,
and if there was a foe, his name was Marshal Ney.

Gold domes were filling eyes of cops with yellow light;
a small plot gave you birth, the nest you lived and died in.
If anything at all went up sky-high then,
it was no railroad bridge but Pavlova in flight.

How splendid late at night, Old Russia worlds apart,
to watch Baryshnikov, his talent still as forceful!
The effort of the calf, the quivering of the torso
rotating round its axis, start

a flight such as the soul has yearned for from the fates,
as old maids cherish dreams while turning into bitches.
And as for where in space and time one's toe end touches,
well, earth is hard all over; try the States.

*1976  /  Translated by Alan Myers with the author*

[ 77 ]

# On the Death of Zhukov

Columns of grandsons, stiff at attention;
gun carriage, coffin, riderless horse.
Wind brings no sound of their glorious Russian
trumpets, their weeping trumpets of war.
Splendid regalia deck out the corpse:
thundering Zhukov rolls toward death's mansion.

As a commander, making walls crumble,
he held a sword less sharp than his foe's.
Brilliant maneuvers across Volga flatlands
set him with Hannibal. And his last days
found him, like Pompey, fallen and humbled—
like Belisarius banned and disgraced.

How much dark blood, soldier's blood, did he spill then
on alien fields? Did he weep for his men?
As he lay dying, did he recall them—
swathed in civilian white sheets at the end?
He gives no answer. What will he tell them,
meeting in hell? "We were fighting to win."

Zhukov's right arm, which once was enlisted
in a just cause, will battle no more.
Sleep! Russian history holds, as is fitting,
space for the exploits of those who, though bold,
marching triumphant through foreign cities,
trembled in terror when they came home.

Marshal! These words will be swallowed by Lethe,
utterly lost, like your rough soldier's boots.
Still, take this tribute, though it is little,
to one who somehow—here I speak truth
plain and aloud—has saved our embattled
homeland. Drum, beat! And shriek out, bullfinch fife!

*London, 1974  /  Translated by George L. Kline*

# Mexican Divertimento

[ *For Octavio Paz* ]

## Cuernavaca

### I

Beneath the tree where M., the Frenchmen's pet,
possessed his pearl of sluggish Indian blood,
a poet sits, who's come here from afar.
The garden's dense, like jewels closely set.
A thrush, like eyebrows knit, departs for food.
The evening air's a crystal chandelier.

The crystal, be it noted, smashed to sand.
When M. reigned here as emperor three years,
he introduced them: crystal, champagne, dancing.
For things like that pep up the daily round.
But then appeared the patriot musketeers
and shot poor M. A doleful, haunting

cry of the crane drifts out from dense blue shadows.
The local lads shake down a rain of pears.
Three snow-white ducks are swimming in the pond.
The ear picks out among the rustling shudders
of leaves the lingo tossed around as pairs
of souls converse in hell of things profound.

### II

Dismiss the palms, let plane trees loom in view.
Imagine M. now laying down his pen;
he flings aside his silken gown and frets
and cogitates on what his kin would do—
Franz Joseph, fellow ruler over men—
and whistles plaintively: "Me and my marmot friend."

"Warm greetings, sir, from Mexico. My wife
went off her head in Paris. Now the palace
walls all resound with shooting, fire sprawls.

Now rebels, brother, choke the city's life.
(My marmot friend and I, we saw the places  . . .)
Well, here guns are more in vogue than plows—

and who's to wonder; tertiary limestone
is just like brimstone, a heartbreaking soil.
Just add to that the equatorial heat.
So bullets are a natural ventilation.
Both lungs and kidneys sense this as they toil.
My skin is sliding off me—how I sweat!

Aside from which, I feel like coming home.
I miss the homeland slums, the homeland splendor.
Send current almanacs—I long for them!
This place will likely prove a goodly tomb
for me and for my marmot. Gorgeous sends her
due greetings to my royal brother. M."

### III

July's conclusion merges with the rains
as talkers get entangled with their thoughts
—a thing of rather small concern to you;
back there the past means more than what remains.
A guitar twangs. The streets are out of sorts.
A passer-by gets soaked and fades from view.

And everything's grown over, pond included.
Grass snakes and lizards swarm here, the tree crowns
bear flocks of birds, some laying eggs, some eggless.
What ruins all the dynasties, blue-blooded,
is surplus heirs replete with numbered thrones.
The woods encroach, and likewise the elections.

M. wouldn't know the place again. Each niche
is bustless now, the colonnade looks bundled,
and walls are sliding slack-jawed down the cliffs.
The gaze is sated, thoughts refuse to mesh.
The gardens and the parks become a jungle.
And "Cancer!" is what bursts out from the lips.

## 1867

Nocturnal gardens under slowly ripening mangoes.
M. dances what one day will be a tango.
His shadow twirls the way a boomerang does
    and the temperature's an armpit 98.
The iridescent flicker of a silver waistcoat;
and a mulatto girl melts lovingly like chocolate
while in a masculine embrace she purrs insensate,
    here—soft as wool, there—smooth as plate.

Nocturnal silence underneath the virgin forest.
Juárez, now the spearhead of, say, progress,
to his peons who never saw two pesos
    distributes rifles in the dark of night.
Bolts start their clicking, while Juárez on squared paper
puts little crosses, ticking off each happy taker.
A gaudy parrot, one who never makes mistakes or
    lies, sits on a bough and notes their plight:

Scorn for one's neighbor among those who sniff the roses
may be, not better, but more straight than civic poses.
But either thing gives quite a rise to blood and bruises.
    Worse in the tropics, here, where death, alas,
spreads rather quickly in the way flies spread infection,
or as a bon mot in a café draws attention,
where three-eyed skulls among the thickets rate no mention;
    in every socket— a clump of grass.

## Mérida

A fan of palms surrounding
a tawny-colored town,
ancient tiles and gables.
Starting from the café, evening
moves into town. Sits down
at a deserted table.

In the ultramarine sky
now touched with golden tints
bells assault the ear

like a bundle of keys:
a sound, laden with hints
of comfort for the homeless here.

A point lights up close by
the cathedral's lofty tower—
Hesperus appearing.
Following it with his eye
filled to the brim with doubt
if not reproach, evening

downs his cup to the lees
(his cheekbones a touch florid),
pays the bill, adjusts
his hat brim over his eyes,
rises from his chair, unhurried,
and folds up his mussed

paper and leaves. The deserted
street makes to accompany
his lean black frame
through the somber mist. A concert
of shadows seems to waylay
him beneath an awning—a lame

rabble: plebeian manners,
blots, tattered loops and dents.
He throws off an onerous:
"Officers, gentlemen.
Betake yourselves hence.
The time is now upon us.

No time to lose, away!
You there, colonel, why, pray tell, is
onion on your breath?"
He untethers his dapple-gray
and gallops off at zealous
clip into the West.

## Mexican Romancero

### I

Good old Mexico City.
Marvelous place to kill an
evening. The heart is empty;
but Time still flows like tequila.

Façades, car flashes, faces
cut in half with mustaches.
The Ave. of Reforma forces
eyes to prefer the statues.

Under each one, in the gutter
with hands stretched to the traffic,
sits a Mexican mother
with her baby. A tragic

sight. Let the winning party
carve them both for a Statue
of Mexico, huge and portly.
To cast some shade in the future.

### II

Something inside went slightly
wrong, so to speak—off course.
Muttering "God Almighty,"
I hear my own voice.

Thus you dirty the pages
to stop an instant that's fair,
automatically gazing
at yourself from nowhere.

This is, Father in Heaven,
a sad by-product of practice,
copper change for the given,
though it's been given gratis.

How far all this is from prayer.
Words cure no despair.
But a fish blind with hunger
can't tell the worm from the angler.

[ 83 ]

### III

Palms, cactus, agaves. Slowly
sun rises where night has stored it.
Its smile—you might find it lovely,
but on a closer look, morbid.

Burned-out boulders. Gritty
soil, as fertile as a bolide.
Sun has a look of grinning
skull. And its rays are bonelike.

Naked-necked vultures carry on
their watch from a telegraph pole,
like hieroglyphs for carrion
in the dust-beaten scroll

of a highway. Turn right,
cactus will catch your sight.
The same on the left. And dead
rusty junk straight ahead.

### IV

Good old Mexico City.
Delights in vocal power.
The band without any pity
grinds out "Guadalajara."

Enter this town. Enter
this mixture of styles and manners
of an unknown painter
framed by the heavy mountains.

Night. Coca-Cola's burning
message adorns the House
of Lawmaking. Beyond it
the Guardian Angel hovers.

Here he runs a risk
of being shot at random
and pinned to an obelisk
as a symbol of Freedom.

## V

Heat retreats from the willow
to a single palm tree.
(I knew I existed while you
were near me.)

A fountain. A pockmarked, fine
nymph lends to its purr her ear.
(I saw all things in profile
while you were near.)

Tabernacles; the zero
of my thinking of Thee
grows. (Who was always there
when you were near me?)

A purple moon in its climb.
A quarter shrunk to a dime.
Midnight. (I didn't fear
dying while you were near.)

## VI

Spreading itself out at last,
like delirium in dust,
the dirt road, sloping gently down,
brings you to Laredo town.

With your blood-swollen eyes,
wedging the knees as does
el toro to thrill a crowd,
you'll sag to the ground.

Life has no meaning. Or
it's just too long. The bore
of arguing lack of sense
stays with us, like that tense

of calendars on the wall.
Very useful. For all
plants, boulders, planets, etc.
Not for bipeds.

## To Evgeny

*In all the elements man is*
*but tyrant, prisoner, or traitor . . .*
—Pushkin

I've been in Mexico, clambered up the pyramids.
Geometrically perfect solids,
dotted here and there on Tehuantepec isthmus.
I hope they really are the work of alien visitors,
since normally such things are raised by slaves alone.
And the isthmus is strewn with mushrooms made of stone.

Little gods of clay who let themselves be copied
with extraordinary ease, permitting heterodoxy.
Bas-reliefs with sundry scenes, complete with writhing bits
of serpent bodies and the mysterious alphabet
of a tongue which never needed a word for "or."
What would they say if they could speak once more?

Nothing at all. At best, talk of triumphs snatched
over some adjoining tribe of men, smashed
skulls. Or how pouring blood into bowls
sacred to the Sun God strengthens the latter's bowels;
how sacrifice of eight young and strong men before dark
guarantees a sunrise more surely than the lark.

Better syphilis after all, better the orifice
of Cortés' unicorns, than sacrifice like this.
If fate assigns your carcass to the vultures' rage
let the murderer be a murderer, not a sage.
Anyway, how would they ever, had it
not been for the Spaniards, have learned of what really happened.

Life is a drag, Evgeny mine. Wherever you go,
everywhere dumbness and cruelty come up and say, "Hello,
here we are!" And they creep into verse, as it were.
"In all the elements . . ." as the poet has said elsewhere.
Didn't he see quite far, stuck in the northern mud?
In every latitude, let me add.

## Encyclopedia Entry

Magnificent and beggar land.
It's bounded on the west and east by beaches
of two blue oceans. In between are mountains,
thick forests, limestone plains, plateaus,
and peasant hovels. To the south lie jungles
and ruins of majestic pyramids.
Lying to the north, plantations, cowboys,
shading quite haplessly into the U.S.A.
Permitting us to dwell awhile on trade.

The chief exports here are marijuana,
non-ferrous metals, an average grade of coffee,
cigars that bear the proud name Corona,
and trinkets made by local arts and crafts.
(Clouds, I must add.) The imports are
the usual stuff and, naturally, rifles.
Possessing a sufficiency of these,
it's somewhat easier to take on the state structure.

The country's history is sad; however,
unique is not the word to use. The main
disaster was, as they insist, the Spaniards,
the barbarous destruction of the ancient
Aztec civilization—that's the local,
plain version of the Golden Horde complex.
With this distinction, namely, that the Spaniards
did grab, in fact, their little pile of gold.

It's a republic now. A nice tricolor
flag flutters high above the presidential
palazzo. The constitution is beyond
reproach. The text with traces of leapfrogging
dictators lies enshrined within
the National Library, secure beneath green bullet-
proof glass—it should be noted, the very same
as fitted in the President's Rolls-Royce.

Which permits us a glance clean through it to
the future. In the future, population,

beyond a doubt, will keep on growing. Peons
will rhythmically ply the hoe
beneath the scorching sun. A man in specs
will sadly leaf through Marx in coffee bars.
And a small lizard on a boulder, raising
its little head, will passively observe
up there in the blue
                              a spaceship's passage.

*1975  /  Translated by Alan Myers with the author*

# The Thames at Chelsea

### I

November. The sun, having risen on an empty stomach,
hovers in a chemist's window on jars of soda.
The wind encounters a hurtle in every subject:
chimneys, trees, a man driven over the tarmac.
Gulls keep a vigil on fences, sparrows peck at the ground.
A transport without wheels crawls over the Thames
as though on a gray, idly wandering road.
Toward the right bank Thomas More aims
his eyes with the age-old desire and strains his mind.
The dull stare is itself more solid than the iron
of the Albert Bridge, and, to put it tersely,
it's the best way of getting out of Chelsea.

### II

The endless street, making a sharp slant,
runs to the river, ending with an iron arrow.
The body scatters its steps on the walk from its rumpled pants,
and trees stand queuing up for the narrow
sturgeonlike waves; that's the only type
of fish the Thames ever is fit to offer.
A local rain darkens Agrippa's water pipe.
A man able to see a century into the future
would view a sooted portico
unspoiled by a pub sign hanging down below,
a line of barges, an ensemble of monotonous
drainpipe flutes, and, at the Tate, an omnibus.

### III

London town's fine, especially in the rain,
which is not to be stopped by cloth caps or crowns.
In this climate only those who make
umbrellas have a chance to seize the throne.
On a gray day, when even a shadow has no strength
to catch up with your back, and the money is getting tight,

in a city where, dark as the brick may get,
the milk will always stand sedately white,
scanning the paper, one may read with care
the account of someone fallen under a car
and only the mention of the relatives' grief
makes one sigh "Well, it's not me" with relief.


IV

These words were dictated to me not by
love or the Muse but by a searching, dull
voice that had lost the swiftness of sound. I
replied, facing my bedroom wall:
"How did you live in those years?" "Like the 'h' in 'oh-oh.' "
"Would you describe your concerns?" "The price of a decent loaf."
"What in the world do you love most?"
"Rivers and streets—the long things of life."
"Do you remember the past?" "Yes, it was winter.
I went for a sleigh ride, caught a cold from the air."
"Are you afraid of death?" "No, it's the normal dark,
but even when you're used to it, you can't make out a chair."


V

The air lives a life that is not ours
to understand; it lives its own blue
windy life that starts overhead and soars
upward, ending nowhere. Looking out of the window, you
see spires and chimneys, rooftops of lead;
you see this: the beginning of a great, damp world
where a roadway, which reared us, heads
to its own premature end. Dawn curls
over the horizon. A mail truck clangs by.
There is no longer anything one can choose
to believe, except that while there's a bank on the right,
there's a left one, too: blessed news.


VI

London town's fine, the clocks run on time.
The heart can only lose a length to Big Ben.
The Thames runs to the sea, swollen like a vein,
and tugs strain their basses in Chelsea. London's fine.
If not in height, then in breadth it lumbers

as boundlessly as it can down by the river.
And when you sleep, the telephone numbers
of your past and present blend to produce a figure—
astronomical. And your finger turning the dial
of the winter moon finds the colorless, vile
chirp, "Engaged," and this steady noise
is clearer than God's own voice.

*1974 / Translated by David Rigsbee*

# A Part of Speech

---

I was born and grew up in the Baltic marshland
by zinc-gray breakers that always marched on
in twos. Hence all rhymes, hence that wan flat voice
that ripples between them like hair still moist,
if it ripples at all. Propped on a pallid elbow,
the helix picks out of them no sea rumble
but a clap of canvas, of shutters, of hands, a kettle
on the burner, boiling—lastly, the seagull's metal
cry. What keeps hearts from falseness in this flat region
is that there is nowhere to hide and plenty of room for vision.
Only sound needs echo and dreads its lack.
A glance is accustomed to no glance back.

The North buckles metal, glass it won't harm;
teaches the throat to say, "Let me in."
I was raised by the cold that, to warm my palm,
gathered my fingers around a pen.

Freezing, I see the red sun that sets
behind oceans, and there is no soul
in sight. Either my heel slips on ice, or the globe itself
arches sharply under my sole.

And in my throat, where a boring tale
or tea, or laughter should be the norm,
snow grows all the louder and "Farewell!"
darkens like Scott wrapped in a polar storm.

From nowhere with love the enth of Marchember sir
sweetie respected darling but in the end
it's irrelevant who for memory won't restore
features not yours and no one's devoted friend
greets you from this fifth last part of earth
resting on whalelike backs of cowherding boys
I loved you better than angels and Him Himself
and am farther off due to that from you than I am from both
of them now late at night in the sleeping vale
in the little township up to its doorknobs in
snow writhing upon the stale
sheets for the whole matter's skin-
deep I'm howling "youuu" through my pillow dike
many seas away that are milling nearer
with my limbs in the dark playing your double like
an insanity-stricken mirror.

A list of some observations. In a corner, it's warm.
A glance leaves an imprint on anything it's dwelt on.
Water is glass's most public form.
Man is more frightening than his skeleton.
A nowhere winter evening with wine. A black
porch resists an osier's stiff assaults.
Fixed on an elbow, the body bulks
like a glacier's debris, a moraine of sorts.
A millennium hence, they'll no doubt expose
a fossil bivalve propped behind this gauze
cloth, with the print of lips under the print of fringe,
mumbling "Good night" to a window hinge.

I recognize this wind battering the limp grass
that submits to it as they did to the Tartar mass.
I recognize this leaf splayed in the roadside mud
like a prince empurpled in his own blood.
Fanning wet arrows that blow aslant
the cheek of a wooden hut in another land,
autumn tells, like geese by their flying call,
a tear by its face. And as I roll
my eyes to the ceiling, I chant herein
not the lay of that eager man's campaign
but utter your Kazakh name which till now was stored
in my throat as a password into the Horde.

A navy-blue dawn in a frosted pane
recalls yellow streetlamps in the snow-piled lane,
icy pathways, crossroads, drifts on either hand,
a jostling cloakroom in Europe's eastern end.
"Hannibal . . ." drones on there, a worn-out motor,
parallel bars in the gym reek with armpit odor;
as for that scary blackboard you failed to see through,
it has stayed just as black. And its reverse side, too.
Silvery hoarfrost has transformed the rattling bell
into crystal. As regards all that parallel-
line stuff, it's turned out true and bone-clad, indeed.
Don't want to get up now. And never did.

You've forgotten that village lost in the rows and rows
of swamp in a pine-wooded territory where no scarecrows
ever stand in orchards: the crops aren't worth it,
and the roads are also just ditches and brushwood surface.
Old Nastasya is dead, I take it, and Pesterev, too, for sure,
and if not, he's sitting drunk in the cellar or
is making something out of the headboard of our bed:
a wicket gate, say, or some kind of shed.
And in winter they're chopping wood, and turnips is all they live on,
and a star blinks from all the smoke in the frosty heaven,
and no bride in chintz at the window, but dust's gray craft,
plus the emptiness where once we loved.

In the little town out of which death sprawled over the
     classroom map
the cobblestones shine like scales that coat a carp,
on the secular chestnut tree melting candles hung,
and a cast-iron lion pines for a good harangue.
Through the much laundered, pale window gauze
woundlike carnations and *kirchen* needles ooze;
a tram rattles far off, as in days of yore,
but no one gets off at the stadium any more.
The real end of the war is a sweet blonde's frock
across a Viennese armchair's fragile back
while the humming winged silver bullets fly,
taking lives southward, in mid-July.

*Munich*

As for the stars, they are always on.
That is, one appears, then others adorn the inklike
sphere. That's the best way from there to look upon
here: well after hours, blinking.
The sky looks better when they are off.
Though, with them, the conquest of space is quicker.
Provided you haven't got to move
from the bare veranda and squeaking rocker.
As one spacecraft pilot has said, his face
half sunk in the shadow, it seems there is
no life anywhere, and a thoughtful gaze
can be rested on none of these.

Near the ocean, by candlelight. Scattered farms,
fields overrun with sorrel, lucerne, and clover.
Toward nightfall, the body, like Shiva, grows extra arms
reaching out yearningly to a lover.
A mouse rustles through grass. An owl drops down.
Suddenly creaking rafters expand a second.
One sleeps more soundly in a wooden town,
since you dream these days only of things that happened.
There's a smell of fresh fish. An armchair's profile
is glued to the wall. The gauze is too limp to bulk at
the slightest breeze. And a ray of the moon, meanwhile,
draws up the tide like a slipping blanket.

The Laocoön of a tree, casting the mountain weight
off his shoulders, wraps them in an immense
cloud. From a promontory, wind gushes in. A voice
pitches high, keeping words on a string of sense.
Rain surges down; its ropes twisted into lumps,
lash, like the bather's shoulders, the naked backs of these
hills. The Medhibernian Sea stirs round colonnaded stumps
like a salt tongue behind broken teeth.
The heart, however grown savage, still beats for two.
Every good boy deserves fingers to indicate
that beyond today there is always a static to-
morrow, like a subject's shadowy predicate.

If anything's to be praised, it's most likely how
the west wind becomes the east wind, when a frozen bough
sways leftward, voicing its creaking protests,
and your cough flies across the Great Plains to Dakota's forests.
At noon, shouldering a shotgun, fire at what may well
be a rabbit in snowfields, so that a shell
widens the breach between the pen that puts up these limping
awkward lines and the creature leaving
real tracks in the white. On occasion the head combines
its existence with that of a hand, not to fetch more lines
but to cup an ear under the pouring slur
of their common voice. Like a new centaur.

There is always a possibility left—to let
yourself out to the street whose brown length
will soothe the eye with doorways, the slender forking
of willows, the patchwork puddles, with simply walking.
The hair on my gourd is stirred by a breeze
and the street, in distance, tapering to a V, is
like a face to a chin; and a barking puppy
flies out of a gateway like crumpled paper.
A street. Some houses, let's say,
are better than others. To take one item,
some have richer windows. What's more, if you go insane,
it won't happen, at least, inside them.

. . . and when "the future" is uttered, swarms of mice
rush out of the Russian language and gnaw a piece
of ripened memory which is twice
as hole-ridden as real cheese.
After all these years it hardly matters who
or what stands in the corner, hidden by heavy drapes,
and your mind resounds not with a seraphic "doh,"
only their rustle. Life, that no one dares
to appraise, like that gift horse's mouth,
bares its teeth in a grin at each
encounter. What gets left of a man amounts
to a part. To his spoken part. To a part of speech.

Not that I am losing my grip: I am just tired of summer.
You reach for a shirt in a drawer and the day is wasted.
If only winter were here for snow to smother
all these streets, these humans; but first, the blasted
green. I would sleep in my clothes or just pluck a borrowed
book, while what's left of the year's slack rhythm,
like a dog abandoning its blind owner,
crosses the road at the usual zebra. Freedom
is when you forget the spelling of the tyrant's name
and your mouth's saliva is sweeter than Persian pie,
and though your brain is wrung tight as the horn of a ram
nothing drops from your pale-blue eye.

*1975–76  /  Translated by the author*

# Lullaby of Cape Cod

[ *For A.B.* ]

### I

The eastern tip of the Empire dives into night;
cicadas fall silent over some empty lawn;
on classic pediments inscriptions dim from the sight
as a finial cross darkens and then is gone
like the nearly empty bottle on the table.
From the empty street's patrol car a refrain
of Ray Charles' keyboard tinkles away like rain.

Crawling to a vacant beach from the vast wet
of ocean, a crab digs into sand laced with sea lather
and sleeps. A giant clock on a brick tower
rattles its scissors. The face is drenched with sweat.
The streetlamps glisten in the stifling weather,
formally spaced,
like white shirt buttons open to the waist.

It's stifling. The eye's guided by a blinking stop light
in its journey to the whiskey across the room
on the nightstand. The heart stops dead a moment, but its dull boom
goes on, and the blood, on pilgrimage gone forth,
comes back to a crossroad. The body, like an upright,
rolled-up road map, lifts an eyebrow in the North.

It's strange to think of surviving, but that's what happened.
Dust settles on furnishings, and a car bends length
around corners in spite of Euclid. And the deepened
darkness makes up for the absence of people, of voices,
and so forth, and alters them, by its cunning and strength,
not to deserters, to ones who have taken flight,
but rather to those now disappeared from sight.

It's stifling. And the thick leaves' rasping sound
is enough all by itself to make you sweat.
What seems to be a small dot in the dark

[ 107 ]

:ould only be one thing—a star. On the deserted ground
)f a basketball court a vagrant bird has set
ts fragile egg in the steel hoop's raveled net.
There's a smell of mint now, and of mignonette.

II

Like a despotic Sheik, who can be untrue
:o his vast seraglio and multiple desires
)nly with a harem altogether new,
varied and numerous, I have switched Empires.
A step dictated by the acrid, live
odor of burning carried on the air
from all four quarters (a time for silent prayer!)
and, from the crow's high vantage point, from five.

Like a snake charmer, like the Pied Piper of old,
playing my flute I passed the green janissaries,
my testes sensing their poleaxe's sinister cold,
as when one wades into water. And then with the brine
of sea-water sharpness filling, flooding the mouth,
I crossed the line

and sailed into muttony clouds. Below me curled
serpentine rivers, roads bloomed with dust, ricks yellowed,
and everywhere in that diminished world,
in formal opposition, near and far,
lined up like print in a book about to close,
armies rehearsed their games in balanced rows
and cities all went dark as caviar.

And then the darkness thickened. All lights fled,
a turbine droned, a head ached rhythmically,
and space backed up like a crab, time surged ahead
into first place, and streaming westwardly,
seemed to be heading home, void of all light,
soiling its garments with the tar of night.

I fell asleep. When I awoke to the day,
magnetic north had strengthened its deadly pull.
I beheld new heavens, I beheld the earth made new.
It lay
turning to dust, as flat things always do.

[ 108 ]

Being itself the essence of all things,
solitude teaches essentials. How gratefully the skin
receives the leathery coolness of its chair.
Meanwhile, my arm, off in the dark somewhere,
goes wooden in sympathetic brotherhood
with the chair's listless arm of oaken wood.
A glowing oaken grain
covers the tiny bones of the joints. And the brain
knocks like the glass's ice cube tinkling.

It's stifling. On a pool hall's steps, in a dim glow,
somebody striking a match rescues his face
of an old black man from the enfolding dark
for a flaring moment. The white-toothed portico
of the District Courthouse sinks in the thickened lace
of foliage, and awaits the random search
of passing headlights. High up on its perch,

like the fiery warning at Belshazzar's Feast,
the inscription *Coca-Cola* hums in red.
In the Country Club's unweeded flower bed
a fountain whispers its secrets. Unable to rouse
a simple tirralirra in these dull boughs,
a strengthless breeze rustles the tattered, creased
news of the world, its obsolete events,
against an improvised, unlikely fence

of iron bedsteads. It's stifling. Leaning on his rifle,
the Unknown Soldier grows even more unknown.
Against a concrete jetty, in dull repose
a trawler scrapes the rusty bridge of its nose.
A weary, buzzing ventilator mills
the U.S.A.'s hot air with metal gills.

Like a carried-over number in addition,
the sea comes up in the dark
and on the beach it leaves its delible mark,
and the unvarying, diastolic motion,
the repetitious, drugged sway of the ocean,
cradles a splinter adrift for a million years.

If you step sideways off the pier's
edge, you'll continue to fall toward those tides
for a long, long time, your hands stiff at your sides,
but you will make no splash.


IV

The change of Empires is intimately tied
to the hum of words, the soft, fricative spray
of spittle in the act of speech, the whole
sum of Lobachevsky's angles, the strange way
that parallels may unwittingly collide
by casual chance someday
as longitudes contrive to meet at the pole.

And the change is linked as well to the chopping of wood,
to the tattered lining of life turned inside out
and thereby changed to a garment dry and good
(to tweed in winter, linen in a heat spell),
and the brain's kernel hardening in its shell.

In general, of all our organs the eye
alone retains its elasticity,
pliant, adaptive as a dream or wish.
For the change of Empires is linked with far-flung sight,
with the long gaze cast across the ocean's tide
(somewhere within us lives a dormant fish),
and the mirror's revelation that the part in your hair
that you meticulously placed on the left side
mysteriously shows up on the right,

linked to weak gums, to heartburn brought about
by a diet unfamiliar and alien,
to the intense blankness, to the pristine white
of the mind, which corresponds to the plain, small
blank page of letter paper on which you write.
But now the giddy pen
points out resemblances, for after all

the device in your hand is the same old pen and ink
as before, the woodland plants exhibit no change
of leafage, and the same old bombers range

the clouds toward who knows what
precisely chosen, carefully targeted spot.
And what you really need now is a drink.

                         v
New England towns seem much as if they were cast
ashore along its coastline, beached by a flood
tide, and shining in darkness mile after mile
with imbricate, speckled scales of shingle and tile,
like schools of sleeping fish hauled in by the vast
nets of a continent that was first discovered
by herring and by cod. But neither cod

nor herring have had any noble statues raised
in their honor, even though the memorial date
could be comfortably omitted. As for the great
flag of the place, it bears no blazon or mark
of the first fish-founder among its parallel bars,
and as Louis Sullivan might perhaps have said,
seen in the dark,
it looks like a sketch of towers thrust among stars.

Stifling. A man on his porch has wound a towel
around his throat. A pitiful, small moth
batters the window screen and bounces off
like a bullet that Nature has zeroed in on itself
from an invisible ambush,
aiming for some improbable bull's-eye
right smack in the middle of July.

Because watches keep ticking, pain washes away
with the years. If time picks up the knack
of panacea, it's because time can't abide
being rushed, or finally turns insomniac.
And walking or swimming, the dreams of one hemisphere (heads)
swarm with the nightmares, the dark, sinister play
of its opposite (tails), its double, its underside.

Stifling. Great motionless plants. A distant bark.
A nodding head now jerks itself upright
to keep faces and phone numbers from sliding into the dark

and off the precarious edge of memory.
In genuine tragedy
it's not the fine hero that finally dies, it seems,
but, from constant wear and tear, night after night,
the old stage set itself, giving way at the seams.


VI

Since it's too late by now to say goodbye
and expect from time and space any reply
except an echo that sounds like "Here's your tip,"
pseudo-majestic, cubing every chance
word that escapes the lip,
I write in a sort of trance,

I write these words out blindly, the scrivening hand
attempting to outstrip
by a second the "How come?"
that at any moment might escape the lip,
the same lip of the writer,
and sail away into night, there to expand
by geometrical progress, *und so weiter.*

I write from an Empire whose enormous flanks
extend beneath the sea. Having sampled two
oceans as well as continents, I feel that I know
what the globe itself must feel: there's nowhere to go.
Elsewhere is nothing more than a far-flung strew
of stars, burning away.

Better to use a telescope to see
a snail self-sealed to the underside of a leaf.
I always used to regard "infinity"
as the art of splitting a liter into three
equal components with a couple of friends
without a drop left over. Not, through a lens,
an aggregate of miles without relief.

Night. A cuckoo wheezes in the Waldorf-
Inglorious. The legions close their ranks
and, leaning against cohorts, sleep upright.
Circuses pile against fora. High in the night
above the bare blueprint of an empty court,

like a lost tennis ball, the moon regards its court,
a chess queen's dream, spare, parqueted, formal and bright.
There's no life without furniture.

VII

Only a corner cordoned off and laced
by dusty cobwebs may properly be called
right-angled; only after the musketry of applause
and bravos does the actor rise from the dead;
only when the fulcrum is solidly placed
can a person lift, by Archimedean laws,
the weight of this world. And only that body whose weight
is balanced at right angles to the floor
can manage to walk about and navigate.

Stifling. There's a cockroach mob in the stadium
of the zinc washbasin, crowding around the old
corpse of a dried-up sponge. Turning its crown,
a bronze faucet, like Caesar's laureled head,
deposes upon the living and the dead
a merciless column of water in which they drown.

The little bubble beads inside my glass
look like the holes in cheese.
No doubt that gravity holds sway,
just as upon a solid mass,
over such small transparencies as these.
And its accelerating waterfall
(thirty-two feet per sec per sec) refracts
as does a ray of light in human clay.

Only the stacked white china on the stove
could look so much like a squashed, collapsed pagoda.
Space lends itself just to repeatable things,
roses, for instance. If you see one alone,
you instantly see two. The bright corona,
the crimson petals abuzz, acrawl with wings
of dragonflies, of wasps and bees with stings.

Stifling. Even the shadow on the wall,
servile and weak as it is, still mimics the rise
of the hand that wipes the forehead's sweat. The smell

of old body is even clearer now
than body's outline. Thought loses its defined
edges, and the frazzled mind
goes soft in its soup-bone skull. No one is here
to set the proper focus of your eyes.


VIII

Preserve these words against a time of cold,
a day of fear: man survives like a fish,
stranded, beached, but intent
on adapting itself to some deep, cellular wish,
wriggling toward bushes, forming hinged leg-struts, then
to depart (leaving a track like the scrawl of a pen)
for the interior, the heart of the continent.

Full-breasted sphinxes there are, and lions winged
like fanged and mythic birds.
Angels in white, as well, and nymphs of the sea.
To one who shoulders the vast obscurity
of darkness and heavy heat (may one add, grief?)
they are more cherished than the concentric, ringed
zeros that ripple outward from dropped words.

Even space itself, where there's nowhere to sit down,
declines, like a star in its ether, its cold sky.
Yet just because shoes exist and the foot is shod
some surface will always be there, some place to stand,
a portion of dry land.
And its brinks and beaches will be enchanted by
the soft song of the cod:

"Time is far greater than space. Space is a thing.
Whereas time is, in essence, the thought, the conscious dream
of a thing. And life itself is a variety
of time. The carp and bream
are its clots and distillates. As are even more stark
and elemental things, including the sea
wave and the firmament of the dry land.
Including death, that punctuation mark.

At times, in that chaos, that piling up of days,
the sound of a single word rings in the ear,

some brief, syllabic cry,
like 'love,' perhaps, or possibly merely 'hi!'
But before I can make it out, static or haze
trouble the scanning lines that undulate
and wave like the loosened ripples of your hair."

IX

Man broods over his life like night above a lamp.
At certain moments a thought takes leave of one
of the brain's hemispheres, and slips, as a bedsheet might,
from under the restless sleeper's body clamp,
revealing who-knows-what-under-the-sun.
Unquestionably, night

is a bulky thing, but not so infinite
as to engross both lobes. By slow degrees
the Africa of the brain, its Europe, the Asian mass of it,
as well as other prominences in its crowded seas,
creaking on their axis, turn a wrinkled cheek
toward the electric heron with its lightbulb of a beak.

Behold: Aladdin says "Sesame!" and presto! there's a golden trove.
Caesar calls for his Brutus down the dark forum's colonnades.
In the jade pavilion a nightingale serenades
the Mandarin on the delicate theme of love.
A young girl rocks a cradle in the lamp's arena of light.
A naked Papuan leg keeps up a boogie-woogie beat.

Stifling. And so, cold knees tucked snug against the night,
it comes to you all at once, there in the bed,
that this is marriage. That beyond the customs sheds
across dozens of borders there turns upon its side
a body you now share nothing with, unless
it be the ocean's bottom, hidden from sight,
and the experience of nakedness.

Nevertheless, you won't get up together.
Because, while it may be light way over there,
the dark still governs in your hemisphere.
One solar source has never been enough
to serve two average bodies, not since the time
God glued the world together in its prime.
The light has never been enough.

## X

I notice a sleeve's hem, as my eyes fall,
and an elbow bending itself. Coordinates show
my location as paradise, that sovereign, blessed
place where all purpose and longing is set at rest.
This is a planet without vistas, with no
converging lines, with no prospects at all.

Touch the table corner, touch the sharp nib of the pen
with your fingertip: you can tell such things could hurt.
And yet the paradise of the inert
resides in pointedness;
whereas in the lives of men
it is fleeting, a misty, mutable excess
that will not come again.

I find myself, as it were, on a mountain peak.
Beyond me there is  . . .  Chronos and thin air.
Preserve these words. The paradise men seek
is a dead end, a worn-out, battered cape
bent into crooked shape,
a cone, a finial cap, a steel ship's bow
from which the lookout never shouts, "Land ho!"

All you can tell for certain is the time.
That said, there's nothing left but to police
the revolving hands. The eye drowns silently
in the clockface as in a broad, bottomless sea.
In paradise all clocks refuse to chime
for fear they might, in striking, disturb the peace.

Double all absences, multiply by two
whatever's missing, and you'll have some clue
to what it's like here. A number, in any case,
is also a word and, as such, a device
or gesture that melts away without a trace,
like a small cube of ice.

Great issues leave a trail of words behind,
free form as clouds of treetops, rigid as dates

of the year. So, too, decked out in a paper hat,
the body viewing the ocean. It is selfless, flat
as a mirror as it stands in the darkness there.
Upon its face, just as within its mind,
nothing but spreading ripples anywhere.

Consisting of love, of dirty words, a blend
of ashes, the fear of death, the fragile case
of the bone, and the groin's jeopardy, an erect
body at seaside is the foreskin of space,
letting semen through. His cheek tear-silver-flecked,
man juts forth into Time; man is his own end.

The eastern end of the Empire dives into night—
throat-high in darkness. The coil of the inner ear,
like a snail's helix, faithfully repeats
spirals of words in which it seems to hear
a voice of its own, and this tends to incite
the vocal cords, but it doesn't help you see.
In the realm of Time, no precipice creates
an echo's formal, answering symmetry.

Stifling. Only when lying flat on your back
can you launch, with a sigh, your dry speech toward those mute,
infinite regions above. With a soft sigh.
But the thought of the land's vastness, your own minute
size in comparison, swings you forth and back
from wall to wall, like a cradle's rockabye.

Therefore, sleep well. Sweet dreams. Knit up that sleeve.
Sleep as those only do who have gone pee-pee.
Countries get snared in maps, never shake free
of their net of latitudes. Don't ask who's there
if you think the door is creaking. Never believe
the person who might reply and claim he's there.

### XII

The door is creaking. A cod stands at the sill.
He asks for a drink, naturally, for God's sake.
You can't refuse a traveler a nip.
You indicate to him which road to take,

a winding highway, and wish him a good trip.
He takes his leave, but his identical

twin has got a salesman's foot in the door.
(The two fish are as duplicate as glasses.)
All night a school of them come visiting.
But people who make their homes along the shore
know how to sleep, have learned how to ignore
the measured tread of these approaching masses.

Sleep. The land beyond you is not round.
It is merely long, with various dip and mound,
its ups and downs. Far longer is the sea.
At times, like a wrinkled forehead, it displays
a rolling wave. And longer still than these
is the strand of matching beads of countless days;

and nights; and beyond these, the blindfold mist,
angels in paradise, demons down in hell.
And longer a hundredfold than all of this
are the thoughts of life, the solitary thought
of death. And ten times that, longer than all,
the queer, vertiginous thought of Nothingness.

But the eye can't see that far. In fact, it must
close down its lid to catch a glimpse of things.
Only this way—in sleep—can the eye adjust
to proper vision. Whatever may be in store,
for good or ill, in the dreams that such sleep brings
depends on the sleeper. A cod stands at the door.

*1975  /  Translated by Anthony Hecht*

# December in Florence

*"He has not returned to his old Florence,*
*even after having died . . ."*
—Anna Akhmatova

### I

The doors take in air, exhale steam; you, however, won't
be back to the shallowed Arno where, like a new kind
of quadruped, idle couples follow the river bend.
Doors bang, beasts hit the slabs. Indeed,
the atmosphere of this city retains a bit
of the dark forest. It
is a beautiful city where at certain age
one simply raises the collar to disengage
from passing humans and dulls the gaze.

### II

Sunk in raw twilight, the pupil blinks but gulps
the memory-numbing pills of opaque streetlamps.
Yards off from where the Signoria looms,
the doorway, centuries later, suggests the best
cause of expulsion: one can't exist
by a volcano and show no fist,
though it won't unclench when its owner dies.
For death is always a second Florence in terms of size
and its architecture of Paradise.

### III

Cats check at noon under benches to see if the shadows are
black, while the Old Bridge ( new after repair ),
where Cellini is peering at the hills' blue glare,
buzzes with heavy trading in bric-a-brac.
Flotsam is combed by the arching brick.
And the passing beauty's loose golden lock,
as she rummages through the hawkers' herd,
flares up suddenly under the arcade
like an angelic vestige in the kingdom of the dark-haired.

## IV

A man gets reduced to pen's rustle on paper, to
wedges, ringlets of letters, and also, due
to the slippery surface, to commas and full stops. True,
often, in some common word, the unwitting pen
strays into drawing—while tackling an
"M"—some eyebrows: ink is more honest than
blood. And a face, with moist words inside
out to dry what has just been said,
smirks like the crumpled paper absorbed by shade.

## V

Quays resemble stalled trains. The damp
yellow palazzi are sunk in the earth waist-down.
A shape in an overcoat braves the dank
mouth of a gateway, mounts the decrepit, flat,
worn-out molars toward their red, inflamed
palate with its sure-as-fate
number 16. Voiceless, instilling fright,
a little bell in the end prompts a rasping "Wait!"
Two old crones let you in, each looks like the figure 8.

## VI

In a dusty café, in the shade of your cap,
eyes pick out frescoes, nymphs, cupids on their way up.
In a cage, making up for the sour terza-rima crop,
a seedy goldfinch juggles his sharp cadenza.
A chance ray of sunlight splattering the palazzo
and the sacristy where lies Lorenzo
pierces thick blinds and titillates the veinous
filthy marble, tubs of snow-white verbena;
and the bird's ablaze within his wire Ravenna.

## VII

Taking in air, exhaling steam, the doors
slam shut in Florence. One or two lives one yearns
for (which is up to that faith of yours)—
some night in the first one you learn that love
doesn't move the stars (or the moon) enough.
For it divides things in two, in half.
Like the cash in your dreams. Like your idle fears

of dying. If love were to shift the gears
of the southern stars, they'd run to their virgin spheres.


VIII

The stone nest resounds with a piercing squeal
of brakes. Intersections scare your skull
like crossed bones. In the low December sky
the gigantic egg laid there by Brunelleschi
jerks a tear from an eye experienced in the blessed
domes. A traffic policeman briskly
throws his hand in the air like a letter X.
Loudspeakers bark about rising tax.
Oh, the obstinate leaving that "living" masks!


IX

There are cities one won't see again. The sun
throws its gold at their frozen windows. But all the same
there is no entry, no proper sum.
There are always six bridges spanning the sluggish river.
There are places where lips touched lips for the first time ever,
or pen pressed paper with real fervor.
There are arcades, colonnades, iron idols that blur your lens.
There the streetcar's multitudes, jostling, dense,
speak in the tongue of a man who's departed thence.

*1976  /  Translated by the author*

# In England

[ *For Diana and Alan Myers* ]

## Brighton Rock

And so you are returning, livid flush of early dusk. The chalk
Sussex rocks fling seaward the smell of dry grass and
a long shadow, like some black useless thing. The rippling
sea hurls landward the roar of the incoming surge and
scraps of ultramarine. From the coupling of the splash of
needless water and needless dark arise, sharply
etched against the sky, spires of churches, sheer
rock faces, these livid summer dusks, the color
of landed fish; and I revive. In the bushes, a careless
linnet cries. The horizon's clean-cut clothesline
has a single cloud pegged out upon it, like a shirt,
and a tanker's masts dip and sway, like an ant
fallen over on its back. Into my mind floats someone's
phone number—the ripped-out mesh
of an empty trawl. A breeze fans my cheek.
The sea swell lulls an anxious splinter,
and a motionless boat lies awash in its reflection.
In the middle of a long or at the end of a short
life, one goes down to the waves not to bathe but for the sake
of that dark-gray, unpeopled, inhuman surface,
as like in color to the eyes, gazing unwinking at it,
as two drops of water. Like silence at a parrot.

## East Finchley

Evening. A bulky body moves quietly along a narrow
walk, with brush-cut hedges and rows of fuchsias
and geraniums, like a dreadnought on a country canal.
His right jacket sleeve, heavily chalk-dusted, betrays
the way he makes his living, as does his very voice:
"You can get away with watering roses and gladioli

somewhat less than dahlias or hyacinths—once or
twice a week." And he quotes me figures from
*The Amateur Gardener's Handbook*
and a line from Vergil. The ground swallows the water
with unexpected haste, and he hides his eyes. In the living room,
sparely furnished, deliberately bare,
his wife—he's been married twice—as befits wives,
lays out, humming, John Galsworthy's favorite patience,
"Spider." On the wall a watercolor: in a river
a bridge is reflected, who knows where.

Anyone living on an island is aware that sooner
or later all this ends: the water in the tap
ceases to be fresh, tastes salty; the foot,
crunching through the gravel and straw, senses
a sudden chill inside the toe end of the boot.
In music there's that place when the record
starts to spin against the moving needle.
On the mantelpiece a stuffed quail looms
that once relied on an infinity of forest,
a vase with a sprig of silver birch,
and a postcard of an Algerian bazaar: heaps
of multicolored stuffs, bronze vessels,
camels somewhere at the back—or is it hills?—
men in turbans. Not like us.

An allegory of memory, embodied in a hard
pencil poised in the air above the crossword.
A house, on a deserted street laid out on a slope,
in whose identical windows the setting sun
reflects as if on those of an express train
heading for an eternity where wheels are not required.
The sweet bedroom (a doll between the pillows)
where she has her "nightmares." The kitchen,
where the gas ring's humming chrysanthemum gives out
the smell of tea. And the outlines of the body
sink into an armchair the way sediment settles in liquid.
Amid the absurdity, horror, ennui of life,
beyond the windows stand the flowers, like tiny
apparel somehow inside out—a rose, symbol
of infinity with its clustered eights,

a dahlia's wheel, spinning between its bamboo bars
like Boccioni's disheveled locomotive,
fuchsia dancers, and, not yet fully open,
irises. Floating in peace, a world
where no one asks, "What's that? What did you say?
Would you repeat that?"—for here the echo
sends the word back unfailingly to the ear
even from as far as the Chinese Wall. Because you
uttered just one word: "Flowers."

## Soho

A massive Venetian mirror holds the opaque profile
of a silk-robed beauty with the crimson wound
of a soundless mouth. The listener scans the walls,
whose pattern has altered over eight years to "Scenes
at Epsom Races." Flags. A jockey in scarlet cap
flies to the winning post on a two-year-old
colt. All merge into one great blur. The stands
go berserk. ". . . didn't reply to my
second letter, so I decided . . ." The voice
is, as it were, a struggle between the verb
and the absent tense. The young, thin hand
ripples the locks that are flowing, falling
into nowhere, like many rivers'
waters. Presently straddling oaken
stallions, two who have fallen heroically in foreign
sheets gallop round the table with its unfinished
bottle toward the gate in what's-it
street. Flags droop down, the wind dies, and drops
of moisture gleam on a rider's lips,
and the stands simply vanish . . . A yellow lamp
burns by the gate, slightly gilding the snowdrifts like
the crumbling crust on a Viennese pastry. No matter who
gets here first, though, in this street the bell
doesn't ring and the hoofs of the gray or the bay
in the present past, even reaching the post, leave no
traces, like carousel horses, on real snow.

## Three Knights

In the old abbey chancel, in the apse, on the floor,
three knights sleep their last sleep, gleaming
in the chancel's gloom like stone sturgeon,
scales of chain-mail, armor-plate gills. All three
hawk-nosed and hatchet-faced, head-to-heel
knights: in breastplate, helmet, long sword. And sleep
longer than they woke. Dusk in the chancel. Arms
crossed on the chest, like carps.

The flash follows the camera's click—a kind
of shot (anything that hurls us forward
onto the wall of the future's a shot). The three,
frozen still, enact once again within
the camera what has already taken place—at Poitiers,
or the Holy Land: a traveler in a straw hat is,
for those who died for Father, Son,
and Holy Ghost, more fearful than the Saracen.

The abbey sprawled at ease along the riverbank.
Clumps of green trees. White butterflies
flutter over flower beds by the chapter house.
The cool of an English noonday. In England, as nowhere else,
nature, rather than diverting, soothes the eye;
and under the chancel wall, as if before
a theater curtain lowered once and for all,
the hawthorn's applause singles out none of them with its call.

## North Kensington

The rustle of an *Irish Times* harried by the wind along
railway tracks to a depot long abandoned,
the crackle of dead wormwood, heralding autumn,
a gray tongue of water close by gums of brick.
How I love these sounds—the sounds of aimless
but continuing life, which for long enough
have been sufficient, aside from the crunch of
my own weighty tread on the gravel. And I fling a bolt skyward.
Only a mouse comprehends the delights of waste ground—

a rusting rail, discarded metal pins,
slack wire, reduced to a husky C-sharp,
the defeat of time in the face of metal.
All beyond repair, no further use.
You can only asphalt it over or blast
it clean off the face of the earth, used by now
to grimacing concrete stadia and their bawling crowds.
Then the mouse will come. Slowly, no rush,
out into the middle of the field, tiny as the soul
is in relation to the flesh, and, raising its
little snout, aghast, will shriek, "What is this place?"

## York: In Memoriam W. H. Auden

The butterflies of northern England dance above
                              the goosefoot
below the brick wall of a dead factory. After Wednesday
comes Thursday, and so on. The sky breathes heat;
the fields burn. The towns give off a smell of striped
cloth, long-wrapped and musty; dahlias die of thirst.
And your voice—"I have known three great poets. Each
one a prize son of a bitch"—sounds in my ears
with disturbing clarity. I slow my steps

and turn to look round. Four years soon
since you died in an Austrian hotel. Under the crossing sign
not a soul: tiled roofs, asphalt, limestone,
poplars. Chester died, too—you know that
only too well. Like beads on a dusty abacus,
sparrows sit solemnly on wires. Nothing so much
transforms a familiar entrance into a crowd of columns
as love for a man, especially when

he's dead. The absence of wind compels taut leaves
to tense their muscles and stir against their will.
The white butterflies' dance is like a storm-tossed ship.
A man takes his own blind alley with him wherever he goes
about the world; and a bent knee, with its obtuse angle,
multiplies the captive perspective,
like a wedge of cranes holding their course
for the south. Like all things moving onward.

The emptiness, swallowing sunlight—something
                        in common with
the hawthorn—grows steadily more palpable
in the outstretched hand's direction, and
the world merges into a long street where others live.
In this sense, it is England. England, in this sense,
still an empire and fully capable—if
you believe the music gurgling like water—
of ruling waves. Or any element, for that matter.

Lately, I've been losing my grip a little: snarl
at my shopwindow reflection; while my finger
dials its number, my hand lets the phone fall.
Closing my eyes, I see an empty boat,
motionless, far out in the bay.
Coming out of the phone booth,
I hear a starling's voice—in its cry alarm.
But before it flies away the sound

melts in the air. Whose blue expanse, innocent of objects,
is much like this life here (where things stand out more
                        in the desert),
for you're not here. And vacuum gradually
fills the landscape. Like flecks of foam,
sheep take their ease on bottle-green waves
of Yorkshire heather. The corps de ballet of nimble
butterflies, taking their cue from an unseen bow,
flicker above a grass-grown ditch, giving the eye

no point of rest. And the willow herb's vertical stalk
is longer than the ancient Roman road,
heading north, forgotten by all at Rome.
Subtracting the greater from the lesser—time from man—
you get words, the remainder, standing out against their
white background more clearly than the body
ever manages to while it lives, though it cry "Catch me!"—

thus the source of love turns into the object of love.

## Stone Villages

The stone-built villages of England.
A cathedral bottled in a pub window.
Cows dispersed across the fields.
Monuments to kings.

A man in a moth-eaten suit
sees a train off, heading, like everything here, for the sea,
smiles at his daughter, leaving for the East.
A whistle blows.

And the endless sky over the tiles
grows bluer as swelling birdsong fills.
And the clearer the song is heard,
the smaller the bird.

*1976  /  Translated by Alan Myers*

# Plato Elaborated

---

I

I should like, Fortunatus, to live in a city where a riv-
er would jut out from under a bridge like a hand from a sleeve,
       and would flow toward the gulf, spreading its fingers
like Chopin, who never shook a fist at anyone as long as he lived.

There would be an Opera House, in which a slightly overripe
tenor would duly descant Mario's arias, keep-
       ing the Tyrant amused. He'd applaud from his loge, but
I from the back rows would hiss through clenched teeth, "You creep."

That city would not lack a yacht club, would not lack
a soccer club. Noting the absence of smoke from the brick
       factory chimneys, I'd know it was Sunday,
and would lurch in a bus across town, clutching a couple of bucks.

I'd twine my voice into the common animal hoot-
ing on that field where what the head begins is finished by the foot.
       Of the myriad laws laid down by Hammurabi
the most important deal with corner kicks, and penalty kicks
                     to boot.

II

I'd want a Library there, and in its empty halls I'd browse
through books containing precisely the same number of commas as
       the dirty words in daily gutter language—
words which haven't yet broken into literary prose. Much less
                  into verse.

There'd be a large Railroad Station in that city—its façade,
damaged in war, would be much more impressive than the outside
       world. Spotting a palm tree in an airline window,
the ape that dozes within me would open its two eyes wide.

And when winter, Fortunatus, threw its coarse shroud over the
                                                                square,
I would wander, yawning, through the Gallery, where
        every canvas, especially those of David and Ingres,
would seem as familiar as any birthmarks are.

From my window, at dusk, I would watch the horde
of bleating automobiles as they flash back and forth
        past shapely nude columns in Doric hairdos,
standing pale and unrebellious on the steps of the City Court.

### III

There would be a café in that city with a quite
decent blancmange, where, if I should ask why
        we need the twentieth century when we already
have the nineteenth, my colleague would stare fixedly at his fork or
                                                                his knife.

Surely there is a street in that city with twin rows of trees,
an entranceway flanked by a nymph's torso, and other things
                                                equally *recherchés;*
        and a portrait would hang in the drawing room, giving
                                                                you an idea
of how the mistress of the house looked in her salad days.

I would hear an unruffled voice calmly treat
of things not related to dinner by candlelight;
        the flickering flames on the hearth, Fortunatus,
would splash crimson stains on a green dress. But finally the fire
                                                        would go out.

Time, which—unlike water—flows horizontally, threading its way
from Friday to Saturday, say,
        would, in the dark of that city, smooth out every wrinkle
and then, in the end, wash its own tracks away.

### IV

And there ought to be monuments there. Not only the bronze riders
                                I would know by name—
men who have thrust their feet into History's stirrups to tame
        History—I would know the names of the stallions also,
considering the stamp which the latter came

to brand the inhabitants with. A cigarette glued
to my lip, walking home well past midnight, I would conjecture
                                                  aloud—
     like some gypsy parsing an open palm, between hiccups,
reading the cracks in the asphalt—what fate the lifeline of the city
                                                  showed.

And when they would finally arrest me for espionage,
for subversive activity, vagrancy, for *ménage*
     *à trois*, and the crowd, boiling around me, would bellow,
poking me with their work-roughened forefingers, "Outsider!
                         We'll settle your hash!"—

then I would secretly smile, and say to myself, "See,
this is your chance to find out, in Act Three,
          how it looks from the inside—you've stared long enough
                                        at the outside—
so take note of every detail as you shout, '*Vive la Patrie!*' "

*1977 / Translated by George L. Kline*

# Letters from the Ming Dynasty

## I

Soon it will be thirteen years since the nightingale
fluttered out of its cage and vanished. And, at nightfall,
the Emperor washes down his medicine with the blood
of another tailor, then, propped on silk pillows, turns on a jeweled
                                                              bird
that lulls him with its level, identical song.
It's this sort of anniversary, odd-numbered, wrong,
that we celebrate these days in our "Land-under-Heaven."
The special mirror that smooths wrinkles even
costs more every year. Our small garden is choked with weeds.
The sky, too, is pierced by spires like pins in the shoulder blades
of someone so sick that his back is all we're allowed to see,
and whenever I talk about astronomy
to the Emperor's son, he begins to joke . . .
This letter to you, Beloved, from your Wild Duck
is brushed onto scented rice paper given me by the Empress.
Lately there is no rice but the flow of rice paper is endless.

## II

"A thousand-li-long road starts with the first step," as
the proverb goes. Pity the road home does
not depend on that same step. It exceeds ten times
a thousand li, especially counting from zeros.
One thousand li, two thousand li—
a thousand means "Thou shalt not ever see
thy native place." And the meaninglessness, like a plague,
leaps from words onto numbers, onto zeros especially.

Wind blows us westward like the yellow tares
from a dried pod, there where the Wall towers.
Against it man's figure is ugly and stiff as a frightening
                                          hieroglyph,
as any illegible scripture at which one stares.
This pull in one direction only has made

me something elongated, like a horse's head,
and all the body should do is spent by its shadow
rustling across the wild barley's withered blade.

*1977 / Translated by Derek Walcott*

# The Rustle of Acacias

Summertime, the cities empty. Saturdays, holidays
drive people out of town. The evenings weigh
you down. Troops could be marched in at even pace.
And only when you call a girlfriend on the phone,
who's not yet headed south and is still at home,
do you prick up your ears—laughter, an international drone—

and softly lay the phone down: the city and the regime
are fallen; the stop lights more and more often gleam
with the red. Picking up a newspaper, you read it from
where "Doing the Town" spills its microscopic type.
Ibsen is leaden. A. P. Chekhov is trite.
Better go for a stroll, to work up an appetite.

The sun always sets behind the TV tower. The West
is right there—where ladies are frequently in distress,
where gents fire six-shooters and say, "Get lost!"
when they're asked for money. There "Man Oh Man"
climbs from a silver clarinet fluttering in black hands.
The bar is a window opened onto those lands.

A pyramid of full bottles has a New York chic;
that sight alone will give you a kick.
What reveals it's the Orient, though, is the bleak, oblique
cuneiform of your thoughts, a blind alley each—
and the banknotes either with Mohammed or with his mountain
                                                         peak
and a hissing into your ear of a passionate "Do you speak . . ."

And when, after, you weave homeward, it's the pincer device,
a new Cannae where, voiding his great insides
in the bathroom, at 4:00 a.m., with his eyes
goggling out at you from the oval mirror
above the washbasin, and gripping his very near
sword, "Cha-cha-cha" utters the new conqueror.

*1977  /  Translated by Daniel Weissbort with the author*

# Elegy: for Robert Lowell

---

### I

In the autumnal blue
of your church-hooded New
England, the porcupine
sharpens its golden needles
against Bostonian bricks
to a point of needless
blinding shine.

White foam kneels and breaks
on the altar. People's
eyes glitter inside
the church like pebbles
splashed by the tide.

What is Salvation, since
a tear magnifies like glass
a future perfect tense?
The choir, time and again,
sings in the key of the Cross
of Our Father's gain,
which is but our loss.

There will be a lot,
a lot of Almighty Lord,
but not so much as a shred
of your flesh. When man dies
the wardrobe gapes instead.
We acquire the idle state
of your jackets and ties.

### II

On the Charles's bank
dark, crowding, printed letters
surround their sealed tongue.

A child, commalike, loiters
among dresses and pants
of vowels and consonants

that don't make a word. The lack
of pen spells
their uselessness. And the black

Cadillac sails
through the screaming police sirens
like a new Odysseus keeping silence.

### III

Planes at Logan thunder
off from the brown mass
of industrial tundra
with its bureaucratic moss.

Huge autoherds graze
on gray, convoluted, flat
stripes shining with grease
like an updated flag.

Shoals of cod and eel
that discovered this land before
Vikings or Spaniards still
beset the shore.

In the republic of ends
and means that counts each deed
poetry represents
the minority of the dead.

Now you become a part
of the inanimate, plain
terra of disregard
of the common pain.

### IV

You knew far more
of death than he ever will

learn about you or
dare to reveal.

It might feel like an old
dark place with no match
to strike, where each word
is trying a latch.

Under this roof
flesh adopts all
the invisibility of
lingering soul.

In the sky with the false
song of the weathercock
your bell tolls
—a ceaseless alarm clock.

*1977*

# Strophes

---

### I

Like a glass whose imprint
leaves a circular crown
on the tablecloth of the ocean
which can't be shouted down,
the sun has gone to another
hemisphere where none
but the fish in the water
are ever left alone.

### II

In the evening here it's
warm. The silence is
completed literally, dearest,
by a parrot's speechlessness.
Into the shrubs of celandine
the moon pours its milk:
far away, in outline,
a body's inviolable silk.

### III

Dearest, what's the point of
arguing over the past
which, in its own turn, is over.
The needle's forever lost
in the human haystack,
not to be found in there.
Feels like hitting a shadow
or—moving your queen on a square.

### IV

All that we've got together,
what we've called our own,
time, regarding as extras,
like the tide on pebble and stone,

grinds down, now with nurture,
now with a chisel's haste,
to end with a Cycladean sculpture,
with its featureless face.

V

Ah, the smaller the surface,
the more modest the hope
of faithfulness and unselfish
love for this speck or drop.
It may be that a body's loss,
in general, from view
is the vengeance on farsightedness
the landscape thinks its due.

VI

Only space sees self-interest
in a finger pointing afar,
and light has its swiftness
in an empty atmosphere.
So eyes receive their damage,
from how far one looks.
More than they do from old age
or from reading books.

VII

The density of darkness's
harm is identical,
for dark's implied flatness
borrows from the vertical.
Man is only the author
of the tightly clenched fist;
thus spoke the aviator
vanishing into the mist.

VIII

The bleaker things are, for some reason,
the simpler. No more do you
crave for an intermission
like a fiery youth.
The light on the boards, in the stage wings,

grows dim. You walk out right
into the leaves' soft clapping,
into the U.S. night.


IX

Life's a freewheeling vendor:
occiput, penis, knee.
And geography blended
with time equals destiny.
Its power is learned of faster
if the stick drives it in.
You submit to the Fatal Sister
who simply loves to spin.


X

My forehead's withered forget-me-
not twists my dental set.
Like our thirty-third letter
I jib all my life ahead.
You know, dear, all whom anguish
pleads for, those out of reach,
are prey of the laws of language—
periods, commas, speech.


XI

Dearest, there are no unfortunates,
no living and no dead.
All's just a march of consonants
on crooked legs, instead.
The swineherd exaggerated,
obviously, his role;
his pearl, lying there unheeded,
will outlast us all.


XII

True, the more the white's covered
with the scatter of black,
the less the species cares
for its past, for its blank
future. And that they neighbor
just increases the speed

the pen picks up on the paper,
promises little good.

### XIII

You won't receive an answer
if "Where to?" swells your voice,
since all parts of the world are
joined up in the kingdom of ice.
Language possesses a pole, named
"North," where a voice won't hoist
its flag, where the snow finds holes and
cracks in the Elzevir cast.

### XIV

These lines are a doomed endeavor
to save something, to trace,
to turn around. But you never
lie in the same bed twice.
Not even if the chambermaid
forgets to change the sheets;
this isn't Saturn, you won't
land from its ring on your feet.

### XV

From the drab carousel that
Hesiod signs and chides
you get off not where you got
on, but where night decides.
No matter how hard you're rubbing
the dark with your pupils, the Lord's
idea of repetition's
confined to the jibing words.

### XVI

Thus one skewers a morsel
of lamb, rakes the fire up.
I've done my best to immortal-
ize what I failed to keep.
You've done your best to pardon
all my blunderings.
In general, the satyr's song
echoes the rustle of wings.

### XVII

Dearest, we are even.
We are immunized, so to speak,
with each other, as if for
pox in a time of plague.
The object of evil gossip
alone gets a forearm shot
with its consoling chance of
dwindling into a spot.

### XVIII

Ah, for the bounty of sibyls,
the blackmail of future years,
as for the lash of our middle
names, memory, no one cares.
To them belongs, like bundles
to storks, the sick-sweetness of lies.
But as long as forgiveness
and print endure, we're alive.

### XIX

These things will merge together
in the eyes of the crew
peering from their flying saucer
at the motley scene below.
So whatever their mission
is, I suppose it's best
we're apart and their vision
won't be put to the test.

### XX

Well, then, remove the Virgin
from the gold frame; put in
the family snapshot version:
a view of the earth from the moon.
A cousin never came close in
to photograph us two
together, nor did the plainclothesmen.
All had too much to do.

### XXI

More out of place than a mammoth
in a symphony den
is the sight of us both smothered
in the present. Good men
of tomorrow will surely wonder
at such a diluted mix:
a dinosaur's passions rendered
here in the Cyrillic marks.

### XXII

These rambling phrases feature
an old man's twaddle, spew.
At our age, judges issue
stiffer sentences to
criminals, and, by the same token,
to their own fragile bones and teeth.
But the free word has no one
there to get even with.

### XXIII

So we switch lights off in order
to knock over a stool.
All talk about the future
is the same old man's drool.
Better, dearest, to bring
it all to an end, with grace,
helping the darkness along
with the muscles of one's own face.

### XXIV

Here our perspective ends. A pity
that it's so. What extends
is just the winding plenty
of time, of redundant days;
gallops in blinkers of cities,
etc., to the finish in view;
piling up needless words of which
none is about you.

### XXV

Down near the ocean,
a summer night. I feel
the heat like a strange hand's motion
on my skull. Orange peel
stripped from its content withers,
grows hard. And the flies flit
like the priests of Eleusis,
performing their rites over it.

### XXVI

I hear the lime tree whisper,
leaning my head on my hand.
This is worse than the whimper
and the famous bang.
This is worse than the word said
to soothe children after a fall,
because after this there follows
nothing at all.

*1978 / Translated by David McDuff with the author*

# San Pietro

I

Three weeks now and the fog still clings to the white
bell tower of this dull brown quarter
stuck in a deaf-and-dumb corner
of the northern Adriatic. Electric
lights go on burning in the tavern at noon.
Deep-fried yellow tints the pavement
flagstone. Cars at a standstill
fade out of view without starting their engines.
And the end of a sign's not quite legible. Now
it isn't dampness that seeps through the ocher and terra-cotta
but terra-cotta and ocher that seep through the dampness.

Shadow draws sustenance from the light
and responds with Christian rejoicing
as a coat is taken down
from its nail. Shutters have spread their wings
like angels plunged headfirst
into someone else's squabbles. Here and there
scab-encrusted stucco peels off,
exposing inflamed red bricks, and skivvies,
drying for three weeks, have gotten
so attached to the open air and their line
that if someone goes outdoors it's with
nothing on under his jacket, barefooted in his slippers.

Two in the afternoon. A postman's silhouette
takes on sharp definition in a hallway only
to become an instant later a silhouette again.
A bell, as it tolls in the fog,
merely repeats the procedure.
So you automatically glance around
in your own direction—like a random stroller
trying for a better look at a pretty girl's ankles
as she rustles past—but you can't see a thing

except scraps of fog. No wind; only stillness.
Indirection. Around a bend
streetlamps trail off like white ellipses,
followed by nothing but a smell of seaweed
and the outline of a pier. No wind.
And stillness like the whinny of Victor
Emmanuel's never faltering cast-iron mare.

## II

In winter, dusk, as a rule, comes too early—
somewhere external, out there, up above.
Tightly swaddled in tattered gauze,
the hands of the town clock
lag behind the scattered daylight
fading in the distance.
A lodger out for some cigarettes
ten minutes later returns to his room
via the tunnel his own body has
burrowed through the fog.
The continuous drone of an unseen airplane
conjures up the hum of a vacuum
at the far end of a hotel corridor,
then dies away, blotting up the light.
"*Nebbia*," yawns the weatherman;
momentarily, eyelids close
like a clam when a fish swims by
(with the pupil briefly descending
into its mother-of-pearl darkness).
A light bulb framed by an archway looks like
a youngster absorbed in his reading
under the covers; the covers are gathered,
like the toga of a saint in a niche. The present,
our time, bounces off the rusty brick
of the old basilica with a thump, as if
a white leather ball had been slammed against it
by schoolboys after school.

Shabby façades, chipped and pitted,
with no option of standing in profile.
Only the bare calves of curved balusters
animating the tightly shuttered balconies

on which no one—neither heiress nor governess—
has emerged in two hundred years.
Cornices chosen by monsters wedded
in embrace or simply bored to death.
Columns guttering like stearin,
and the blind, agate splendor
of impenetrable glass behind which lurk
a couch and an upright piano:
ancient secrets that are in fact
best kept dark by daylight.

When the weather's cold, normal sound would rather
bask in the warmth of a throat than risk echo's whimsey.
A fish is tight-lipped; deep inland
a turtledove sings its song. But you can't hear
either one. A canal bridge spanning fresh water
keeps the hazy bank on the other side
from breaking away and drifting seaward.
So then, on breath-coated glass, one can trace the initials
of those whose absence is hard to swallow;
and a cherished monogram trickles down
as the tail of a sea horse. Apply that red
sponge of your lungs and soak up the thick milky
mist—the breath of Amphitrite and her Nereids!
Stretch out a hand—and your fingertips
will touch a torso that's flecked with tiny
bubbles and scented with the iodine of childhood.

### III
A swish of ruffles on the washed and ironed
sheet of the bay and, for a moment, colorless air
condenses into a pigeon or a sea gull,
but quickly dissipates. Dinghies, longboats,
gondolas, flatbottoms, hauled from the water,
lie scattered like odd shoes on the sand
creaking underfoot. Remember:
any movement is basically
a shift of body weight from one location
to another. Remember: the past won't fit
into memory without something left over;
it must have a future. And remember carefully:

only water, and it alone,
everywhere and always stays true to it-
self, unsusceptible to metamorphoses, level,
present wherever dry land
is gone. And the inflation of living—
with its beginning, middle, thinning calendar,
end, et cetera—shrinks before
colorless, shallow, eternal ripples.

The rigid, lifeless wire of a grapevine
quivers imperceptibly with its own tension.
Trees in the garden blackness,
indistinguishable from a fence resembling
someone without anything or, more important,
anyone left to confess to.
Twilight. No wind. The stillness.
The crunch of coquina, the rustle of crushed,
moldering reeds. A tin can launched skyward
by the tip of a shoe goes sailing
out of sight, and a minute later
there is still no sound of it falling on
wet sand. Or, for that matter, a splash.

*Venice, 1978 / Translated by Barry Rubin*

# NOTES

## Autumn in Norenskaya

Norenskaya is a village of fourteen dwellings in the Archangel region of the U.S.S.R., where the author temporarily resided in 1964–65.

## A second Christmas

*Pontus:* the Pontus Euxinus, the ancient name of the Black Sea.

## A Song to No Music

*"Tongue of native asps":* This reference to trees in Russia is taken from an epigram by Ivan Turgenev characterizing the language used by a nineteenth-century Russian translator of Shakespeare.

## The End of a Beautiful Era

*Rurik:* a ninth-century Norseman who, according to the Russian *Primary Chronicle*, was invited by the Russian tribes around Novgorod to come and rule and is considered the founder of the first Russian princely dynasty.

## Lithuanian Divertissement

*Liejyklos:* a street in Vilnius ("Foundry Street").
*Vytautas:* Vytautas the Great (*c.* 1350–1430), Grand Prince and most famous monarch of early Lithuania.
*Amicum-philosophum de melancholia, mania et plica polonica:* The Latin title of a medieval manuscript in the Vilnius library, meaning "To a philosopher friend, on madness, melancholy, and plica polonica." According to *Taber's Cyclopedic Medical Dictionary, plica polonica* is "tangled matted hair in which crusts and vermin are embedded."
*Palanga:* renowned Lithuanian seaside resort on the Baltic coast.
*The Dominicans:* a Catholic cathedral in Vilnius.

## Nunc Dimittis

This poem is based on the account in Luke 2:22–36, considered the point of transition from the Old Testament to the New. The title in the original, *Sreten'e* (literally, "The Meeting," referring to Simeon's meeting with the infant Christ), denotes the church festival celebrated as the Feast of the Presentation in the Temple. Simeon's speech in the fifth and sixth stanzas is the *Nunc dimittis* ("Now lettest thou thy servant depart . . .") found in most Christian liturgies. The date of the poem, February 16 (on the New Calendar, or February 3 on the Old), is the Feast Day of Saints Simeon and Anna, and hence the name day of Anna Akhmatova.

### 1972

*Stanza 3:* "Those who'll carry you out besiege the doorway" is a paraphrase of the Apostle Peter's words to Sapphira in Acts 5:9.

*Stanza 4:* "Well met, then, joyful, young, unfamiliar tribe!" is a paraphrase of a line of Pushkin's addressed to a grove of young trees that have sprung up next to three old pines he used to see during his two years in exile.

"*Ivan's queen in her tower*": a motif of Russian folk tales.

*Stanza 6:* "even a cuckoo's crooning in darkness": In Russian folklore, the number of calls emitted by a cuckoo predicts the number of years that a person has left to live.

*Stanza 7:* "metallic brow": The Russian phrase *medny lob* has the figurative meaning of "numskull."

*Stanza 9:* "Dragged my fool": a paraphrase of a standard Russian obscenity.

*Stanza 10:* "Listen, my boon brethren": an echo of Prince Igor's address to his warriors in the *Lay of Igor's Campaign*, the twelfth-century Old Russian epic.

*Stanza 11:* "as with Prince Igor's helmet": In the *Lay*, Igor expresses an urge to drink of the Don from his helmet.

### Lagoon

*VII:* "northern sphinxes of renown": the two sphinxes of King Amenhotep III on the Neva esplanade, in front of the Academy of Arts in Leningrad.

## On the Death of Zhukov

This poem was inspired by Derzhavin's celebrated poem *Snigir'*
("The Bullfinch"), written in May 1800 on the death of Count A. V.
Suvorov, commander of the Russian armies under Catherine the Great.
The bullfinch's song is supposed to resemble the sound of a fife. The
meter of both poems suggests the slow interrupted beat of a military
funeral march.

## Mexican Divertimento

This poem employs meters that are standard in Spanish poetry. In
particular, *1867* is set to the rhythm of "El Choclo," an Argentine
tango; *Mérida* is in the meter used by the fifteenth-century Spanish poet
Jorge Manrique; and *Mexican Romancero* has the traditional poetic
form of the Spanish ballad.
*Cuernavaca, II:* "Me and my marmot friend" is Beethoven's "Marmotte,"
from his Opus 52, set to Goethe's words.
*To Evgeny*, Stanza 4: "Cortés' unicorns" are a type of cannon.

## A Part of Speech

*From nowhere with love:* "resting on whalelike backs": A reference to
the myth that the world is supported on the backs of whales.

## Lullaby of Cape Cod

*II:* "I beheld new heavens, I beheld the earth made new": These lines
are an ironic echo of Isaiah 65:17—"For, behold, I create new heavens,
and a new earth: and the former shall not be remembered, nor come
into mind."
*VIII* (and, again, in *X*): "Preserve these words" is an echo of a Mandel-
stam poem, dedicated and addressed to Anna Akhmatova, which begins,
"Do preserve what I've said for its taste of misfortune and smoke."

## December in Florence

The epigraph is from Akhmatova's poem "Dante."
*IV:* "the unwitting pen strays into drawing—while tackling and 'M'—
some eyebrows" alludes to the medieval notion that facial features repre-
sent letters in the phrase OMO DEI.

## *Elegy: for Robert Lowell*

This poem was written in English.

### *Strophes*

x: "thirty-third letter": In the Russian alphabet the thirty-third letter is Я.